Tick Tock,
It's LYME O'clock

A Warrior's Guide to Reclaiming Health & Happiness

Christa Nannos

Tick Tock, It's LYME O'clock

Formatting by Rik – http://www.WildSeasFormatting.com

Cover Design by 100 Covers – https://100covers.com

Headshot by Erica Blaine Photography featuring Aware Causes necklace

ISBN: 979-8-9851874-0-3

Disclaimer

This book details the author's personal experiences with and opinions about Lyme disease. The author is not a healthcare provider or medical professional.

The author and publisher are providing this book and its contents on an "as is" basis and make no representations or warranties of any kind with respect to this book or its contents. The author and publisher disclaim all such representations and warranties, including for example warranties of merchantability and healthcare for a particular purpose. In addition, the author and publisher do not represent or warrant that the information accessible via this book is complete or wholly current and the author and the publisher will not be liable for any possible damages in connection with the use of this book.

The statements made about products and services have not been evaluated by the U.S. Food and Drug Administration, or any other governmental agency. Consult with your own physician or healthcare specialist regarding the suggestions and recommendations made in this book as this book is not intended as a substitute for consultation with a licensed healthcare practitioner, such as your physician.

Dedication

This book is dedicated to anyone battling an invisible illness. I believe you, I see you, and you are not alone. To the Lyme warrior friends I've met along the way: We've laughed together, cried together, and you've helped me find joy throughout this journey. To the doctors who've helped me heal: Thank you for your guidance, knowledge, and understanding; and for treating me like a person, not a statistic. And last but not least, to my family and friends: Thank you for supporting me, loving me, and never giving up on me. We're all in this together, and this book would not have been possible without each and every one of you.

Contents

Introduction

Hey brave warrior! You've probably picked up this book because you either have Lyme disease, suspect you have Lyme, or know someone who does. Welcome! And thanks for reading. I hope my story will educate, inspire, and motivate you to keep going—no matter what battle you're facing—and help you side-step the trials I faced along the way. And yes, there were many, starting with my diagnosis. I was misdiagnosed for more than a decade and, when I finally received the correct diagnosis, I found recovery to be the greatest challenge of all. This book is therefore a compilation of "things I wish I knew" before I started treatment, "things I learned along the way," and "things people don't talk about" that are vital to know when it comes to healing from this pernicious disease. At the time of this writing, I am not yet in remission. I am still going through multiple treatments, but I am deep into my journey back to health. Everybody's story is unique. I can only speak about my own, but each of us needs to be heard, believed, and treated with respect. And we are *all* worthy of having a happy and fulfilling life. I truly believe that remission is well within my reach, and that it can be for you, too. Please note that this book does not name the doctors, clinics, or programs I've worked with, in order to keep their identities safe—but those details don't matter because what worked and didn't work for me, may or may not be the case for you. There is no "correct" way to heal from Lyme, and this book will show you just how many treatment options exist. In the meantime, we must keep fighting the good fight because better days are ahead for us all!

Lyme disease is an invisible illness. So, for many years, people waved away my concerns by telling me "you look great" because, on the outside, I did. And on certain days, I felt great too. But my health often changed drastically from day to day and, sometimes, hour to hour. Other people couldn't understand why, and I didn't understand either. All I knew was that something was very wrong and that I would keep fighting until I got to the bottom of it. From my suffering, understanding, and in-progress healing from chronic Lyme disease—a condition Western medicine doesn't formally recognize and is said to be under study by the U.S. Health Department—it's my hope that I can be a voice for the voiceless. I want to remind you that no matter what you're going through, your life matters: your symptoms are real, and your feelings are valid. You might feel broken, but you're not—and you deserve a healthy and happy life. Let me walk with you during your dark days, as I open up about the despair I felt. Let me help you feel less alone, though I know just how lonely a chronic illness can actually be. And finally, let me laugh with you when Lyme gets weird because a life without laughter is no life at all. I certainly don't have all the answers, and I don't claim to be an expert— but I have a story, and it's one worth telling. This is my story, and everything I've learned along the way.

Part One: My Story & Healing Journey

The Bite

All it took was one bite, from one tick, to change my life forever. It's true what people say, that the small moments are what define you. And often, it's the moments you had no idea would matter that become the most meaningful. I can't tell you exactly how old I was when I was bit, but I know I was around eight or nine years old. I can't tell you exactly what I was doing, except I know I was playing outside in my backyard. And I can't tell you why not one doctor, in the 10½ years after I became symptomatic, ever tested me for Lyme disease. I *can* tell you that I encountered many ticks growing up, and never thought anything of it. I *can* tell you that I remember the tick that bit me because it took me at least two hours, using my dad's tweezers, to pry it out. (On my first try, I was only able to remove half of it from my thigh. The other half stayed lodged in my skin till after dinner, when I tried again.) I can also tell you that for whatever reason, I did not think to tell my parents what had happened. I remember asking someone on AOL instant messenger, "Can you die from a tick bite?" and they responded, "No."

As you can guess, I didn't save the tick. I didn't get a rash. And I didn't get sick—until I went to Guatemala, a decade later, when I was 19 years old. I was sick from age 19 to age 29, at which point I got the correct diagnosis of Lyme disease. Did you know that Lyme symptoms can be dormant for months, years, or even decades? I sure didn't. But I've learned that all it takes is one stressful event, or exposure to a toxin, to stir things up. In my case, I'm certain I got a parasite while cliff-jumping in Guatemala, despite every infectious disease doctor saying I didn't. But the moment I returned from that trip, I had unexplainable nausea, crippling gastrointestinal (GI) pain, sudden intolerance to certain foods, and extreme fatigue. All tell-tale signs of parasites! And yet no one believed me. I now know those parasites are what triggered my Lyme symptoms.

Misdiagnosis: 2009–2019

I saw over 20 specialists within 10 years, and not a single person thought to test me for Lyme disease even though I grew up in Pennsylvania—which has often been the state with the most Lyme cases per capita—and despite remembering being bit by a tick. I saw both Eastern and Western medical doctors, went to the hospital more times than I can count, had medical procedures I didn't need, and worked with energy healers from all around the world. I did it all…and was told it all. For the longest time, no one believed my symptoms, and then I was variously informed that I had irritable bowel syndrome (IBS), anxiety, tendonitis, Schmorl's nodes (spinal disk herniations), overactive bladder syndrome, candida overgrowth, small intestinal bacteria overgrowth (an abnormal increase of bacteria in the small intestine, often referred to as SIBO) and that my "sex energy was blocked." That last one was the kicker for sure. I was told a vibrator would "cure all of my symptoms"! So, naturally, I bought one. If you would have told me that walking through fire would have cured me, I would have…but no, a vibrator did not magically make my nausea disappear. I wish! At that point in my life, I had been suffering 14 months straight with debilitating nausea and stomach pain. And yet no doctor I saw could figure out why. After 10 years of battling strange food allergies, and trying every diet you can imagine, I continued to get worse. My intense joint pain became crippling, and no amount of physical therapy or rest made any difference. And then the doctor I had been seeing told me, "There's nothing more I can do for you, it's all in your head."

I prayed for healing. I cried, I succumbed, but I never stopped fighting for an answer. But, after 10 years, I finally got one. In fact, even before I tested positive for Lyme, I figured out that that's what I had. I came to this conclusion after talking to others with Lyme disease and comparing our symptoms. This is the case for so many of us. We learn we have Lyme when others share their stories, and we connect the dots ourselves. Maybe my book will help you in this way, or help someone you know. Is Lyme the answer for every misdiagnosis out there? Of course not. But when the Centers for Disease Control (CDC) estimate that nearly 480,000 people get diagnosed with Lyme disease every year (and no one knows how many people go misdiagnosed, like I did)—a number that keeps climbing—it's worth looking into. Lyme disease is often called "The Great Imitator" because it gets misdiagnosed for, and mimics the symptoms of, chronic fatigue syndrome, multiple sclerosis, fibromyalgia, Hashimoto's thyroiditis, Parkinson's disease, rheumatoid arthritis, and more. So, if you battle any of those illnesses, and aren't getting better from treatments, Lyme is something to consider. It's hard, but you must learn to be your biggest advocate on your healing journey.

If you know something is off, don't stop fighting until you get the answers you deserve.

For me, everything started to click after I received the correct diagnosis. It confirmed that this wasn't "all in my head," I wasn't "making this up for attention," and I wasn't "going crazy." It confirmed that everything I had felt for the past decade was REAL. And this chronic illness is very real. If you're still searching for answers, or being told your Lyme results "aren't positive enough," don't give up! Did you know the standard blood test for Lyme (called ELISA) can be roughly 60% inaccurate? No wonder it often takes people multiple doctors, and multiple years, to get diagnosed. But you know your body best, and if something is wrong, something is wrong. If you can't find answers, and your symptoms align with Lyme, find a "Lyme literate" medical doctor (LLMD) in your area, or a naturopath who specializes in Lyme. Your feelings and frustrations are valid, and you deserve to get the correct diagnosis. The medical community truly failed me, and if you feel that way too, I'm so sorry, but things will get better! One day, everything will start to make sense.

For the longest time, I would ask myself, "Why didn't any doctors bring up Lyme disease"? Not only was I not tested, but no one even mentioned it as a potential cause of my symptoms. I was angry, hurt, and felt let down by every single doctor who didn't recognize my diagnosis— one that seems so straightforward to me now! But, at the same time, I started asking myself, "Why didn't I ever ask to be tested"? It turns out I was as uneducated about Lyme disease as all those doctors. Today I ask myself, "Why wasn't I taught about Lyme disease in school?" Ticks are everywhere in Pennsylvania, so why wasn't this spoken about? Well,

I can't turn back time, and I'm certainly not going to put my energy into fighting a broken medical system (at least not right now). Healing is my number one priority, but I'm so glad that I finally got answers after years and years of suffering. Every misdiagnosis wasn't in fact wrong, it just wasn't the root cause of my problems. Lyme disease is, along with parasites; and until I found that out, every treatment I was given was just a Band-Aid for my issues. We have to find the base cause of our ailments, or we will never really get better. I'm grateful to be on the right path, finally, and I know you'll get there too. Stay strong and keep fighting for your health. After all, if you don't do it, who will?

Diagnosis: January 2020

At the start of 2020, I was correctly diagnosed with Lyme disease. Before I got my lab results, I looked at my blood under a darkfield microscope and could actually see the Lyme spirochetes (corkscrew-shaped bacteria) swimming around. There were so, so many. The nurse told me they're "having babies!" and we could see them replicating. It was gross, but at least I was starting to get answers. Then I got my IGeneX bloodwork back. I had so many bands present, including being CDC positive (5 or more bands are present compared to IGeneX criteria of 2 or more bands present), that my doctor exclaimed "you have the most amount of Lyme disease I've seen in a while!" Well, there is no "winner" when it comes to Lyme, but it sure felt like my results put me at the top of a contest I never chose to be a part of. And, despite having a positive CDC test, which I should note is not very common in the chronic Lyme community, the CDC still does not truly recognize or have treatments for chronic Lyme disease. But getting this diagnosis, after a decade of wondering what was going on, was one of the greatest feelings I've ever had. I felt validated! I felt seen. I felt heard. And above all, I finally felt *believed*.

One thing I didn't know, until getting diagnosed, is that there's a lot of judgement surrounding *chronic* Lyme disease. So my first day of real celebration quickly turned into confusion as people began telling me my diagnosis was "fake." Some people think that two weeks of doxycycline eradicates all bacteria, and so chronic Lyme can't exist. Well, taking antibiotics can usually help to cure *acute* Lyme, which typically surfaces soon after being bit by an infected tick. But I was bit more than 20 years before my diagnosis, leaving me untreated that entire time. And my research indicates that antibiotics alone rarely work on chronic Lyme disease, also known as late-stage Lyme. Sometimes, they can even make you worse. It's now known that Lyme bacteria can persist for long periods, and that it can become resistant to antibiotics, making it all the more imperative to seek treatment immediately, if you've been bit. The funny thing is, I did take doxycycline at the beginning of my treatments because I got shingles in my ear. Shingles! And no, doxycycline did not cure my Lyme disease.

All in all, getting diagnosed felt like a miracle after everything I had been through, but my journey was really just beginning, and I had no idea how difficult it was about to get. These next chapters offer a glimpse into my treatments. I could write an entire memoir about my decade-long misdiagnosis and my journey towards remission—in fact I plan to—but for now, you'll gain a better understanding of who I am and the progress I've made, over the past two years, as I've worked to finally address chronic Lyme disease.

Hyperthermia Treatments

Once I was diagnosed with Lyme, I jumped headfirst into a type of immunotherapy (a treatment that targets the immune system, so the body can fight diseases). It's a treatment that induces fever in the patient—which is technically a state of hyperthermia—so I will refer to the practice by using this term from now on.

This protocol—not approved for use in every state—is great at stimulating your mitochondria to help your immune system recognize Lyme bacteria (Borrelia burgdorferi) as a foreign invader, and fight it off (it helps that Lyme bacteria cannot survive in extremely high temperatures). In hindsight, I should have started the healing process with what's known as "parasite cleansing" (more on this in "Toxin Overload"), but I was so ready to get better after more than a decade of suffering, that I chose the first (and very expensive) option I'd heard of to begin. Still, seeking out hyperthermia treatment led me to my first, amazing doctor—a Doctor of Osteopathy (aka, a DO). He was the first professional to treat me traditionally and holistically, and he authentically cared about me getting better. This great DO took the time to get an overall picture of my health, and it was the first time I felt completely seen, heard, and believed. The treatment also gave me my first glimpse of healing. So for that, I will be forever grateful!

I traveled to a clinic where I did a few weeks of detoxification treatments—aka "detox" treatments—a process that removes toxins from the body. I was given a variety of IV treatments including high doses of vitamin C to aid the immune system, phosphatidylcholine for liver support, and hydrogen peroxide to increase oxygen in tissues; painful glyoxal injections (administered to the butt!) also meant to stimulate the body's defense mechanisms to better fight off toxins; and one of several kinds of hyperthermia. I underwent 20 induced, homeopathic fevers, each around 103°. You might know the saying, "you never know how strong you are until strong is your only option." Well, this phrase took on an entirely new meaning for me, during this time. For starters, these treatments stirred up a dormant infection of chickenpox I had as a kid, which became shingles and spread throughout my ear (as I mentioned earlier)…such fun! But that was nothing compared to the pain of hyperthermia. The pain was crippling. I promise you, it would bring the strongest person you know to their knees. But I did these treatments every day, with no break save for Sundays. It was the hardest thing I've ever done. We patients called the hyperthermia "Shake and Bake" because we would get extremely cold, shake uncontrollably, and then our fevers would skyrocket. The fevers would then naturally come down after a few hours, or we'd take medication to bring them down. Yes, this was safe and yes, I was monitored by my doctor and his nursing staff the entire time. My mom was also there with me—thank God for moms!—and I made some incredible Lyme warrior friends who battled alongside me. I felt extremely supported, and I knew I was in good hands. For these reasons, despite enduring the worst physical suffering I've ever experienced, I was known for singing and dancing my way through the fevers.

I sang songs like the Jonas Brothers' "Burnin' Up," Nelly's "Hot in Here," and Shakira's "Hips Don't Lie." What can I say? I bring the comic relief wherever I go! Staying positive is my superpower, and so is laughing out Lyme. I was at that clinic for a total of six weeks and, when I left, my blood was free of Lyme spirochetes! I wasn't surprised because I could feel myself healing as the days wore on. And, as you can imagine, I was super excited to get back to Los Angeles and tell all my friends I was *all better*. So, I went home and continued my doctor's orders to detox, and to keep up certain homeopathic injections. I started to get my life back after hyperthermia, but even though I felt better, I did not reach remission. Lyme disease can become dormant, mimicking remission, but I had a few other ailments brewing that would soon reignite the bacteria. Little did I know that my journey was just beginning.

After leaving that clinic and despite many improvements, I was extremely fatigued—though this was expected after everything my body had gone through. But, as I continued to detox at home using my infrared sauna, castor oil packs on my liver, and getting colon hydrotherapy (a bowel system flush also called a colonic) at a local clinic, I started developing new and strange symptoms. I developed Mast Cell Activation Syndrome (MCAS), aka: I was covered in hives, off and on for a few months. I became sensitive to smells, chemical products, and even the sun. My adrenals (glands that produce hormones that help regulate your immune system, metabolism, blood pressure and stress response) were depleted from all the treatments, which caused more fatigue, and my sleep pattern changed, fairly drastically. While I used to suffer from insomnia, I was now falling asleep at 8 p.m., and waking up at 4 a.m. every day, naturally. It was odd. I know now that the hyperthermia treatments stirred up the co-infection Babesia—a microscopic parasite that infects the red blood cells, causing symptoms similar to malaria, and is spread by certain ticks. I developed drenching night sweats (a common symptom), which wasn't anything I'd experienced pre-treatment. It's how I learned that, when you begin to treat Lyme disease, new symptoms can surface, and old ones can often become far worse than they were before. I did not know this going into treatments, because doctors really don't prepare you for these outcomes! Which is also why I'm writing this book. All in all, I came to understand that healing is a lot harder than being sick, and that my journey was just beginning.

Parasites (Round 1)

As the months passed, I continued to feel better but, after staying somewhere that, unbeknownst to me had mold; and battling some of the most debilitating fatigue I'd ever felt; fears that my symptoms matched those of someone with parasites proved true. After doing an intense week-long liver detox that consisted of taking supplements and drinking olive oil, and a series of colonics, my body expelled a parasite all on its own. I was not taking any antiparasitic medications or herbs at that time, yet my body just ejected it one night, into the toilet. I mean, literally ejected it, without stool or anything. It just fell out of my butt! I guess my body had had enough and finally said, "get out!" But that's one thing I've learned: our bodies fight for us, even when we aren't expecting it. Here's what happened: I was in the most amount of pain, even worse than during the hyperthermia treatments, so after an emergency phone call with my Lyme doctor, my friend rushed me to the ER, per his request. When I got there, I remember being bent over the ground, crippled with agony. And, even though no one was in the waiting room, it still took them an hour to see me. Once I finally met with the doctor, he told me, "There's no way you could possibly have parasites." Just like the Infectious Disease doctor told me after I came back from Guatemala 12 years ago but, this time, I had passed a six-inch worm, and even had a picture of it on my phone. He didn't care. Remember when I said the medical system fails Lyme patients? This was another example.

Instead of being taken seriously, I was laughed at. They gave me morphine for the pain, ran a CT scan, and then told me I was constipated. A common misdiagnosis I'd heard frequently over the past years. And, long story short, I've been passing parasites nearly every day since that Emergency Room visit 10 months ago. Worms of different shapes, colors, and sizes. I've taken several different samples to the lab, with technicians exclaiming, "I've never seen a tapeworm in person before!," but the results came back negative. The lab couldn't determine what they were, only that they "were not parasites." Well, I don't know about you, but I call a worm a worm! So, per usual, I led with my own intuition, found some holistic doctors and began to treat for parasites. It was going well, until another virus decided to rear its head, bringing my parasite cleanse to a full stop. This meant stopping the herbs and other supplements before their prescribed duration. And, since I ended these treatments early—as many people do, thinking a cleanse should only last a few weeks when, in reality, parasite cleansing takes months, and sometimes even years—the parasites were not fully eradicated and so they came back with a vengeance later on.

COVID-19

We all know what happened in 2020, right? COVID-19. And in January 2021, one year after getting diagnosed with Lyme, I contracted coronavirus 2, aka, SARS-CoV-2. Just my luck! As if the last year wasn't rough enough, I became of one the millions of victims of this new, worldwide pandemic—alongside the Lyme epidemic, and despite being the girl who wore two masks, goggles, and gloves into CVS. I lost my taste and smell, developed high fevers (which I was a pro now at fighting), had migraines, night sweats, extreme fatigue, swelling in my legs, muscular and joint pain, severe diarrhea, and brain fog. I had delt with each of these symptoms before—except for the loss of taste and smell—but the combination of all of them at once was brutal. Adding to the hardship was the fact that I lived alone and essentially had to fend for myself. Thankfully, some dear friends were able to drop off vitamins and food, and I video-called my family every day. Nonetheless, battling COVID-19 was a lonely and rough time. I'm deeply grateful that I got through it—though, to my misfortune, it stirred up my Lyme disease symptoms to such a degree that I had to immediately return to treatment.

I got retested for Lyme, and my results came back IgG and IgM positive, which means a recent and previous infection. Since I was not re-bitten by a tick, this means that SARS-CoV-2 had simply reactivated my infection. Looking back now, most of my COVID-19 symptoms were symptoms also associated with Lyme, so it's hard to know what was what. But it doesn't matter. All of it was terrible. Oh, and even after I'd recovered, I developed parasomnia, a distortion of smell common to those who've made it through COVID, where previously enjoyable aromas become unpleasant and even intolerable. For me, everything smelled like poop for about six months afterwards! Thankfully, that symptom has gotten better over time. But after I beat COVID-19, I felt I had no choice but to switch gears and focus again on Lyme. And, this time around, I decided to see a local, Lyme literate medical doctor—a well-known such doctor might I add—but the next chapter in my healing journey did not, in the end, turn out well. In fact, it was to be a living nightmare.

More Lyme Treatments

This LLMD came highly recommended, but was not the right doctor for me. I wish I'd had the strength to fire her at the first sign that her protocol wasn't helping but rather hurting me, but I spent the next four weeks in hell. I started IV antibiotics, medical IV ozone (an oxygen treatment used to fight disease), antiparasitic meds, bicillin (a type of antibiotic) butt shots and more. I had severe Herxheimer reactions (Jarisch Herxheimer reactions (JHR), which I'll explain in depth a little later but, in simple terms, are a cluster of severe bodily reactions sustained when Lyme and other toxins die off in your body, causing an overload of symptoms, also known as a Cytokine Storm). After that, I spiraled into a deep depression after being put on an antibiotic with a black box warning for suicidal thoughts—a warning I was not told about. I couldn't think clearly, and therefore could not advocate for myself. I was prescribed B12 stomach injections that caused an allergic reaction, and I was covered in a painful rash for weeks; a rash the doctor did not consider reason enough to stop the treatment. And, one night after taking one of her suggested, detoxifying Epsom salt baths, my skin began to leak black gunk. A black, tar-like substance came oozing out of my pores from my feet to my face. I can laugh now and say I looked like a "Swamp Monster" (because I did) but, back when it was happening, it was one of the most terrifying experiences of my life. I saw this black stuff coming out of me, tried to wipe it off, but it just smeared all over my skin. It was like trying to wipe mascara off without makeup remover. It took me four hours to clean myself off because it kept coming back. This episode was diagnosed as Morgellons Disease (a little-understood condition characterized by skin legions or small fibers emerging from the skin)—but my current medical team believes it was a sign of mold toxicity—so I was put on two more courses of oral antibiotics to treat Morgellons, which only made me sicker.

I hope I'm conveying well enough that this doctor didn't listen to me. She didn't seem to care that I was far worse, four weeks on, than when I began. And she wasn't available when I needed her most. I sent her emails asking for advice when I was utterly sick, and she responded, "emails are only for emergencies." I was scared, I was desperate for help, and I was alone. And that's when I left her. I like to say I fired her, because you know what?, these doctors work for us, not the other way around. This LLMD opened my eyes to the world of uncaring Lyme doctors. I thought only regular MDs treated their Lyme patients with hostility (because they don't understand Lyme), but I was wrong. Even Lyme literate doctors can be jerks. I learned a lot from this doctor about my own resilience, about the need to trust in myself, and also how important it is to find a doctor who cares. Which was also one of the reasons I was driven to write this book. It's so important to advocate for yourself, but when you're battling chronic Lyme disease, it can be very, very difficult. All in all, I fought, I survived, I left that doctor at the end of that month, and have continued to move forward on my healing journey.

Energy Healing

Trying anew, I decided to take a break from Western medical treatments for a while. I knew I needed to reset, refocus, and give my body the chance to breathe. That's when I began energy healing work. I had worked with many healers in the past, but this was the first time I was truly open to its benefits. I'm grateful to note that this step was a true game changer. I worked with a healer to clear me of food allergies—something this practitioner does remotely, over the phone. Now, before you dismiss this as too "woo woo," I recommend that when it comes to healing, don't knock something until you try it! As it happens, I felt closer to full remission when working with this healer than at any other time and, to this day, I am still under her care.

It needs noting that her treatments have not been easy. Indeed the detox symptoms were well more than I was ready for, more than I'd even anticipated, but it's been worth it. After every energy healing session, I feel different detox symptoms emerge as the food allergies begin exiting my body. The most common symptoms are fatigue, stomach upset, sinus pressure, and swollen glands. But, after 12 years of terrible food allergies and intolerance, I'm finally able to eat nearly everything I want to, again! The biggest and most exciting addition being dairy. I used to fall asleep after eating milk products—as in, borderline passing out—but now I have no issue, whatsoever. And, after years of bloating, pain, nausea, indigestion, constipation, and diarrhea, along with many types of food sensitivities, I believe my GI tract has fully healed. I can say this about only one other treatment, and that's the parasite cleansing. To be even more clear—and this book is meant to be fully transparent—I went from pooping up to five times a day, to one and done! I never thought I'd see a time when I'd be a regular pooper and didn't always need to be on the lookout for a bathroom. Not only has energy healing changed my gut; it's changed my life.

I want to quickly mention another type of energy healing that's helped me a lot over the years, and that's working with a holistic chiropractor who does neurological realignment. This type of chiropractic work is less about cracking body parts, than about realigning the brain-body connection. I began working with this chiropractor a few years before being diagnosed with Lyme disease, and he was able to minimize and even completely eradicate some of my symptoms. I went from taking Advil multiple times a day, to taking no pain medication at all. I was also on Zyrtec, and several other pills for everyday allergies, and with his help I've gotten that down to none. The holistic chiropractor has also helped alleviate both pain and inflammation—and was able to shift my body out of fight-or-flight mode, aka raised cortisol levels, which made a huge difference in how I felt, and my ability to function. All in all, energy healing and holistic treatments have been incredibly effective for me, and so I want to encourage you to be open to all sorts of healing remedies, too. After all, as my experience showed me, the strangest-seeming treatment might be the one that helps you the most.

Parasites (Round 2)

As I mentioned earlier, I am not yet in remission—but I know it's close! Currently, I'm also working with a new practitioner who specializes in parasites. That means I'm back on an intense parasite treatment, which has included a lot of supplements to support my liver, lymphatic system, and drainage pathways (the ones that allow your body to eliminate waste); herbs to kill parasites; and more enemas than you can imagine. That six-inch worm that my body expelled is nothing compared to the 10-foot tapeworm I passed with this practitioner! It came out in three separate segments, over three days, after doing water enemas. Still, it was a horrifying experience. How long was that parasite living inside me?! And how could every stool test for parasites have come back negative when creatures like that were brewing and breeding inside me? I count this as just one more example of how the medical system failed me, but this is not a story of failure—it's one of success and healing. It's also a story of hard work, of never giving up, and of having faith that you'll get better! And I do. This practitioner energetically tests me for parasites, and we've seen my levels drop incredibly fast. I believe that energy healing for allergies and gut health and parasite cleansing, go hand in hand. The more I've been able to fix my gut, the less habitable a place my body is for parasites. Emotional work is also key to passing parasites. I've been doing Mind Body Spirit Release (MBSR)—another type of energy healing—with another practitioner, and I believe that's what allowed the tapeworm to release from my intestinal wall. Again, if this sounds too "woo woo," please don't knock it till you try it! I now have days where I feel 100% healthy because these critters are finally leaving my body. I can't believe people walk around feeling this well, every day!

Finally Starting to Heal

As I finish this book, I'm in the midst of a "Healing Girl Summer." I've dedicated the summer of 2021 to parasite cleansing, resting, and retraining my brain (more about this in "Treatment Options"). After passing gallstones in Los Angeles back in May, and experiencing a highly visceral set of die-off symptoms from parasites, I couldn't live alone anymore. Nor could I support myself. So, my dog and I temporarily moved home to be with my parents this June. At first, I thought of the move as a kind of giving up, but the reality is that I've finally *given in* to healing, and I've never felt better. I've surrendered to the means by which I believe I'm going to heal, and am now truly embracing this journey. Life is like the ocean. We can't control it, but we can ride the waves. My journey is not over, but I've learned a lot along the way. And, if my story can help even one person, it'll be worth the telling. We're all different, but we're all in this together. So remember: never give up! No matter what you're facing, you've got this. I hope you'll ride the waves with me, and may this book help you stay afloat during the storm.

Part Two: Navigating the Medical System

This section covers everything I think you'll need to know when you first begin your Lyme journey. It can also be useful if you haven't gotten better from the treatments you've started, and are looking for more options. I'll discuss everything from the tick bite, to testing, to treatment options, to finding a doctor, and more. May these practical tips about navigating the medical system help guide you on your way!

Prevention: How Not to Get Bit

Let's talk about prevention when it comes to Lyme disease. Protecting ourselves from ticks is extremely important, especially when we're hiking or camping in the woods. But ticks have also been found on beaches, in cities, and basically anywhere outdoors. Did you know that some ticks can be as small as a poppy seed? And that they secrete a saliva with anesthetic properties, so you can't feel the bite, which makes it even more imperative to take the necessary precautions to protect yourself. While this book is directed more toward those who already have Lyme, there are measures we can all take so as not to get bit. These include:

• **Wear tick and bug repellent.** I like less toxic brands like Tick Tock Naturals and Ranger Ready.

• **Wear tall socks.** It's even better if you tuck your pants into your socks. I know it might look strange, but covering up as much as possible will prevent ticks from biting you.

• **Wear white and other light colors** so you can easily spot any ticks that attach themselves to your clothes. And, when you return from time outdoors, throw your clothes in the dryer for 10–15 minutes, which will kill live ticks.

• **Do tick checks daily**. To contrary belief, ticks don't "go away" during the winter. They exist all year long, and they like to bury themselves in hard to see places such as armpits, in between toes, and along your scalp. Ticks have been found in every state and continent, including Antarctica. If you think ticks aren't where you live, please think again—and stay alert!

You Found a Tick, Now What?

Here are 10 steps* I recommend following if you have just been bitten by a tick:

STEP 1: DON'T PANIC. It's normal to be freaked out, but try to stay calm because the next few steps are crucial. Take some deep breaths: When your body is in a state of panic, you can't think clearly.

STEP 2: REMOVE THE TICK. You'll want to use fine-tipped tweezers to get as close to the skin surface as possible. Pinch the tick with the tweezers and pull upwards in a steady motion. If you twist when pulling, the tick's body might break off and the mouth could stay stuck in your body (this happened to me). If this happens, try to get as much of the tick out as possible, and call your doctor or go to an Urgent Care. DO NOT wait for the tick to detach on its own. Ticks can feed on a host for days, and still go unnoticed. Likewise, DO NOT try to burn the tick off, or paint it with nail polish—both erroneous tips you might find online. You *do* need to get it out of your skin and as quickly and safely as possible.

STEP 3: SAVE THE TICK. Put the tick in a Ziploc bag or mason jar. If you do this, you'll be able to send the tick out for testing. Not every tick carries Lyme disease, but they all carry certain viruses and bacteria.

STEP 4: CLEAN THE AREA where the tick bit you. Wash your hands, then clean the area: I suggest doing so with a betadine wipe, immediately followed by an alcohol wipe. I also suggest mixing bentonite clay with some water, and applying the paste to the affected skin. After a few hours, the clay will start to fall off and you can remove the rest with a wipe. After that, you can apply a triple antibiotic gel to the bite location every 12 hours for 3 days. (PLEASE NOTE: Do not use a betadine wipe if you are allergic to iodine, have a thyroid issue, or are pregnant or breastfeeding).

STEP 5: MARK THE AREA & TAKE A PICTURE. Take a pen and draw a circle around the tick bite location. Then take a picture of the circled area, and monitor it for the next few days to see if a rash appears. Absolutely look for the tell-tale bull's-eye rash, but note that sometimes, the rash can look different than that; and know that some people never develop a rash at all (I did not).

STEP 6: WRITE DOWN the day and time the tick bite occurred. Also note your exact location at the time of its occurrence, because certain ticks live in certain areas, and it might help professionals determine the type of tick that bit you.

STEP 7: CALL YOUR DOCTOR and set up an immediate appointment. If your doctor is not concerned about your tick bite, call another practitioner, or visit an Urgent Care center or ER. There are many Lyme literate and holistic doctors you can have a phone consultation with, too. I believe that getting on the right antibiotic or herbal protocol after a tick bite can prevent the infection (if there is one) from becoming chronic.

STEP 8: TAKE A PICTURE OF THE TICK and email it to Tick Encounter Resource Center for a free tick report. Their website is https://web.uri.edu/tickencounter.

STEP 9: MAIL THE TICK to a trustworthy tick testing service. Ticknetics Tick Testing Laboratory is a good company, and the Bay Area Lyme Foundation has a lot more information on this as well. You can also call your local vector control office.

STEP 10: MONITOR YOUR SYMPTOMS. Take note of how you feel each day for the next few weeks-to-months, and continue to monitor the area where the tick bit you. If you develop symptoms (see next chapter), call your doctor immediately. Don't wait to start treatment. Acute Lyme is curable! Chronic Lyme, as of now, is not. Most doctors prescribe two weeks of doxycycline for acute Lyme, but that is not necessarily long enough to kill all the bacteria. There is no guarantee that antibiotics will work in the first place (about 10% of infections will go on to become chronic) but taking a prescribed course for at least four to six weeks may give you a better shot at curing acute Lyme. Studies have indicated that Lyme bacteria can survive a 28-day course of antibiotics, so you really need to be on the medication for at least that long. There's also no definitive answer on when Lyme goes from the acute stage to the chronic stage. Some say it can shift after even a few weeks without treatment, following a bite; others say it takes a few months, to a year. No matter when the tick bit you, even if it was years ago and you're just reading this now: if you have symptoms, make an appointment with a doctor who understands and acknowledges chronic Lyme.

* Most of this information was sourced from the curators of Tick Boot Camp, Matt Sabatello and Rich Johannesen. You can check out their website at TickBootCamp.com in order to view their Tick Bite Blueprint, see more tips about ticks, and listen to their podcast. The goal of the Tick Boot Camp Podcast is to help people liberate themselves from the suffering caused by Lyme disease.

Common Lyme Symptoms

Once I found out that I had Lyme disease, I had a lot of "Aha!" moments when it came to my symptoms. If you haven't felt that way yet, I hope this information helps you realize that you're not "crazy," and that you most certainly aren't alone. Also note that symptoms can come and go randomly, which is also completely normal for Lyme! Many of these symptoms can also pertain to mold, parasites, heavy metals, and co-infections of Lyme. It therefore may be hard to tease them apart. But, after my decade-plus battle with Lyme; and from my time in the vast Lyme community, spent listening to other Lyme warriors' stories, I've found the list of common Lyme disease symptoms to include:

Nausea

Gastrointestinal issues

Fatigue

Joint pain

Muscle aches

Brain fog

Word confusion

Insomnia

Headaches

Migraines

Seasonal allergies

Food allergies/sensitivities

Temperature intolerance

Night sweats

Dizziness

Vertigo

Mood changes

Anxiety

Trouble focusing

Panic attacks

Depression

Puffy gums

Teeth sensitivity

Eye floaters

Light sensitivity

Hair loss

Tinnitus

Bladder issues

Chest pain

Swollen glands

Stretch marks (on thighs)

Twitching

Sensory overload

Bell's palsy

Impaired perception

Rheumatoid arthritis

Chronic sinus infections

Air hunger (shortness of breath)

Tunnel vision

Swollen eyelids

Neuropathy

Hot flashes

Double vision

TMJ (jaw lock)

Finding a Doctor

There are Lyme literate medical doctors, other medical doctors who treat Lyme, holistic doctors, energy healers, and more. It can be daunting to figure out where to start! As I've already said but can't stress enough, because everyone is different, each Lyme warrior will require different treatments and kinds of doctors. I'll also repeat that I highly recommend getting referrals from people in the Lyme community. Because chronic Lyme is such a controversial disease from the viewpoint of the U.S. medical community, I've found word-of-mouth to be the best way to sort out the good doctors from the bad. If you aren't part of a Lyme community yet, that's okay; there are plenty of other trustworthy resources out there for you. Here's a list of ways I've been able to find my favorite doctors.

1. **Check out one of the many, many groups and organizations dedicated to assisting Lyme warriors**. Most have support groups and resource pages that can help you get plugged into the community. A few of my favorite groups are Tick Boot Camp, Global Lyme Alliance, Generation Lyme, Project Lyme, Sam's Spoons Foundation, LymeLight Foundation, and Ride Out Lyme. And there are so many more! I suggest you contact these organizations directly, or join a support group and ask around about which doctors members have seen, which ones have worked for them, and which ones treated them with respect. It's also worth finding out if these doctors work remotely, or whether you'd need to travel to see them; and whether they take insurance or not (usually not). Either way, having a direct referral

to a Lyme doctor is one of the best places to start.

2. Research and browse social media! Listen to Lyme podcasts and watch Lyme documentaries; and read articles, interviews, and blogs. Hearing someone's firsthand experience with Lyme, and learning which doctors helped them heal, is invaluable. Much like my reasons for writing this book, our stories are what truly help each other the most. And I've gained so much insight from listening to Tick Boot Camp's podcast alone! I've made lists of treatment options, and which doctors to see (as well as who not to see)—just from that podcast. So, I highly recommend listening to their podcast, and podcasts in general!

3. Share your story! Not everyone will feel called to share their story publicly, and I totally understand that, but even sharing your story privately with a few chosen people can help. I discovered that I most likely had Lyme through connecting with a friend of a friend, and I was introduced to my energy healer through a friend of a friend. You never know who someone else might know, and putting yourself out there opens you up to a world of possibilities. Now, you'll also receive unsolicited advice when you do this (which I'll touch on later) but, for better and worse, sharing my story is the reason why I'm finally healing today.

If you suspect you have parasites, mold, or other co-infections, look for doctors (holistic and medical) who treat those conditions, too. Many practitioners will want to treat parasites and mold first, and others have a different plan of attack. I believe it's helpful to treat parasites *before* Lyme because parasites will hold onto Lyme bacteria even when you think it's been eradicated. So, I recommend finding a doctor who will look at your health as a whole, and won't only fixate on Lyme disease. Many people end up needing to see more than one doctor on their healing journey, and that's okay! You don't need to find all your doctors right away! It's best to start with one, and know that whoever you choose isn't likely to handle all your ailments. That might seem stressful but, in reality, I hope it also takes the pressure off of needing to find the "perfect" doctor. No one's perfect. You just need to start somewhere, and with someone you feel understands your case, and makes a good argument for how they'll help you heal.

Preparing for Your Visit

Starting to work with a new doctor can be overwhelming. Rehashing your entire medical history, which might be years' worth of information, is a lot to discuss—and a lot to go through, emotionally. If you haven't already, create a folder, or several, and fill it with the documents, notes, and timelines of your medical history. Or make a software spreadsheet of the information. Many people don't realize that they can ask for copies of their test results, summaries of their appointments, and even a disk loaded with their medical imaging. It's your right to ask for all this, and having your own copy of this information can be really helpful when seeing a new doctor! So, if you haven't done this in the past, I recommend doing so at your next appointment. You can also call previous providers and request this information retroactively! The bottom line is: it's *your* medical history, and having copies of everything will only help you in the future.

Once you've got all of your medical information in one place, organize it in whatever way works best for you. It should include a record of all the doctors you've seen, all the tests you've had—ideally with the most recent information at the front—as well as all the diagnoses you've received, and treatments you've already undergone. Some doctors won't take the time to review this information in advance, but they should be open to discussing anything you bring up during your appointment. This will also save you the hassle and cost of retaking recent blood tests.

I can't stress how important it is for you to organize this information before your appointment or, ask someone to help you organize it. I've spent way too much money retesting for things and doing extra blood work, all because I wasn't clear with my doctor about what I had already or recently had checked. If it's been a few years since a test, a doctor may well ask you to get tested again, and that's fine. Still, it's worth mentioning prior tests because some are prohibitively expensive, and not covered by insurance. For me, all this was a daunting task. My mom certainly kept better records of everything than I did, and I'm so grateful for her help. If you're able, lean on your support system for assistance! Whether that's a family member, spouse, or friend, it's sometimes necessary to ask a buddy to step in.

So, now that you have your information organized, speaking to your doctor requires its own preparation. You'll be asked a ton of questions, so it's helpful to review them at home, ahead of time. The first being, what are your main symptoms? Meaning, your day-to-day struggles. And what are your secondary symptoms? Meaning, things you occasionally experience, but ones that don't affect your daily life. Once you learn more about Lyme disease, and everything it can do to the body, you might realize that you've had symptoms come and go that affected you at the time, but you no longer do. That's normal, but it's worthwhile to take note of them and tell your doctor because it's all important! As I've mentioned before, Lyme symptoms can also go dormant and then return. You might end up realizing you've had Lyme disease for far longer than you thought. Reviewing all this information can be very overwhelming, especially if you're battling brain fog, so I recommend asking your doctor if you can record your session. Having a caretaker, family member, or friend there with you as a second set of ears can really help, too. I would often call my mom, and put her on speaker phone while the doctor explained everything, so my mom could take notes. There's no shame in asking for this help, and I touch on this concept in great detail later on.

But now that you've explained all your symptoms to your doctor, and gone over all of your test results, they'll start to go over their treatment protocol, aka: how they'll "get you to remission." I put that phrase in quotes because doctors are not God. I heard more than 20 doctors tell me they could "cure me," and not one of them did. Not only did those doctors fail to diagnose me with Lyme disease, the two Lyme specialists I saw did not bring me into remission, despite their promises. "Cure" is a word some people throw around, but technically there is no cure for chronic Lyme disease (yet!). Yet many of the doctors I saw, both pre- and post-Lyme diagnosis did help. I don't want to scare you into not trusting your doctor, because it's important that you do, but it's also important to question them, and have them explain exactly what they plan to do, and why.

Here are some questions you should consider asking your doctor:

• May I record this session? And if not, can I have a family member join by phone?

• Why is this the treatment you recommend for *me*?

• Are there any side effects to this treatment?

• How long will this treatment take?

• What is the plan if I start to get worse?

• Is there an emergency number I can use to reach you? Do you have another doctor on-call when you're not available?

• What is this supplement for? When do I take it? And should I take it with or without food?

• Is there anything I should be doing on my own, alongside this treatment?

• Should I be detoxing, or go on any specific diet?

• Will we be treating my adjacent conditions (like mold, heavy metals, and parasites) as well? If so, which do we treat first, and why? And what is the timeframe for the combined treatment?

• Do you take insurance? Or have any kind of payment plan? (Note that prices can get overwhelming, so it's important to be upfront about any financial issues you might have. Some practitioners might be able help you work out a solution, but others may not. You should also find out whether your insurance covers out-of-network doctors and treatments. Either way, you can submit out-of-network bills to your insurance company, yourself. It's a complicated process, but can be worth it in the end.

Basically, it comes down to making sure that your doctor is treating you for your individual case of Lyme disease, rather than for some generic template of Lyme. Every person is different, and will require different treatments. Your doctor should be willing and able to answer all your questions about this and, if they aren't, you need to ask why. Before throwing money their way, make sure you feel confident and comfortable in the treatment plan you've been given. After all, they work for *you*. Which means you're the boss; remember that.

Testing for Lyme

I know from experience that testing for Lyme disease is difficult because many tests are inaccurate, and a lot of Western doctors don't believe chronic Lyme disease exists. Also, most people think you only get Lyme disease if you develop the bull's-eye rash. Well, studies have shown that only about 40% of people develop this rash, and it might even be less than that. I did not get one. And remember, the standard antibody blood test for Lyme, the ELISA blood test, can be inaccurate some 60% of the time because it can take weeks to develop Lyme antibodies. Despite this, the ELISA blood test is the primary test doctors run when a patient has just been bit by a tick. So, not only are tests unreliable, but doctors don't even think to test for Lyme unless you have that rash—again, one that not everyone develops, and that can look very different from person to person, and depending on skin tone. I hope this changes in the future. That being said, I still recommend getting tested! Some doctors can diagnose you based on your symptoms and a lot of people, like me, actually come to realize they have Lyme after speaking with a friend or someone else who has Lyme disease. Dr. Richard I. Horowitz even has a free online quiz (you can find it at DoYouHaveLyme.com) that can help determine if you have Lyme! But getting that positive blood test changed my life, and it might change yours, too. I realize now that having some sort of "proof" that I had Lyme made a big difference to me—and to my family and friends. Still, as I've said, not everyone gets a positive blood test, even though they have Lyme disease. So don't be discouraged if you haven't tested positive yet. You know your body best. And keep advocating for yourself.

Here's a list of the best labs and tests that I know of that can help diagnose Lyme disease. It's so important that we educate ourselves as much as we can, because we cannot simply rely on doctors to have all the answers—especially since so many doctors I saw didn't test me for Lyme. That being said, I encourage you to work with a doctor to determine the test that is right for you, but also know that there are many options available.

- IGeneX

- The Western blot (a qualitative blood test in which antibodies for Borrelia burgdorferi antigens are visualized)

- Creating Balanced Health

- ArminLabs

- DNA ConneXions

- Galaxy Diagnostics

- Vibrant Wellness

- Fry Laboratories

- Bioenergetic Testing

- RED Laboratories

- Herbal Provocation (a 3-week process of taking herbs prior to a blood test can help determine which infections you have, based on your response to the herbs)

- Medical Diagnostic Laboratories

You Have Lyme, Now What?

First, *hallelujah* to the doctor (or whoever it was) who correctly diagnosed you! It feels so good to finally have answers, and for everything you've gone through to be validated. Take this day to have a mini celebration because today, you are one step closer to remission! But here's the thing…a lot of people don't recognize that chronic Lyme disease exists. So, after months, or years, of people not believing you, you might find yourself in a similar position once again. But don't let anyone else's opinion sway you from continuing to seek out help. And try your hardest to surround yourself with people who believe you and support you.

The world is changing, and more and more people are recognizing how debilitating Lyme disease is, but there will always be deniers and haters, no matter what the issue is. I've had family members continue to doubt my diagnosis, and had friendships ruined because some people just weren't able to support me once I had been formally diagnosed with a chronic illness. I'm here to say that this is okay. Well, it's really not okay, but this is the time for you to build your support system, or "Lyme Team," if you will. Healing is physically, mentally, emotionally, and spiritually challenging, so there is no room in your life for drama or doubters. Some of your relationships might just need to be paused for the time being, and perhaps later down the road you can connect again. But at the end of the day, I can't stress enough how important it is for you to put yourself first and really commit to your journey, in order to heal.

You likely already know that you're not the same person you were before you got Lyme disease. What you may not know is that you are now a warrior, and you are going to come out stronger because of this battle. It might not feel this way every day, but it's true. When your physical symptoms amplify, and they often will, you may feel like you've completely lost control of your body. But try to remember that your mind is growing stronger and more resilient, and you'll become grateful for every healthy day you have. Many of my Lyme friends, myself included, have mourned the person we were before becoming chronically ill. It's completely natural to feel this way. No one wants to get Lyme disease, and change can be really scary. As I've already said: healing is hard work—but now you've entered into a special "club" of people who are truly the strongest people I've ever known. Lyme does not and will never define you, but how you live with it, and fight for your health, will. This means it's time to re-evaluate your doctors, support system, and lifestyle so you can create the most healing environment possible. Lyme literate doctors are really important, but not every doctor will be right for everyone. The thing is, there's no one answer! Everyone's path is different, but I encourage you to really do your research before choosing the members of your healing team. I recommend asking around in several Lyme communities, seeking out referrals, looking up practitioner's reviews, and inquiring as to whether you can have a consultation before committing to anything new. Likewise, take a look at your friendships, and see who's been there for you during your worst times, and who was only there when you were feeling great. Cutting out toxic relationships, and those that are unfulfilling—at least for the time being—can be crucial to your healing. And if you're living an unhealthy lifestyle—think, partying all the time, eating junk food, and not getting enough sleep—you need to make some changes, ASAP. Everyone is different, and I'm certainly not going to tell you how to live your life, but once you're able to put your own health and welfare first, you'll be able to start the process of conquering this disease.

Treatments & Doctors

There are so many treatment options to choose from, but note that many are extremely expensive, and what works for someone you know, or who you met in the Lyme community, is not guaranteed to work for you. That's why I can't tell you what you should do. I'm not a doctor, just one person who's lived with this disease. I can, however, describe for you the different treatment options I know of—though it's vital that you do your own research, and seek out a knowledgeable professional's opinion, before trying any of them. The same goes for doctors. Just like dating, it may take some looking to find the right fit, and knowing that ahead might save you a lot of time and energy. As I've tried to describe, I've gone down the wrong path time and time again. But I've learned from these experiences, so if you find yourself in a similar situation, give yourself grace. You're doing your best, and that's all you can ever do!

Another thing I wish I'd known at the beginning of my healing journey, is that treatments are either going to work with your body to fight Lyme disease, or against your body. And both may happen to you, too. But you won't know until you try. Unfortunately, it usually takes a lot of trial and error, but that's where having a good doctor comes in. By now you've probably heard the phrase, "you get worse before you better," applied to how people heal from Lyme disease. The statement is true, to a degree, but there's also only so much your body can take. I'm extremely sensitive to medications, so I've learned that I have to take things really slowly. Some people can go, go, go—no matter how hard the treatments get—and others, like me, need to focus on supporting and building up their immune systems before eradicating anything from their body. Again, there is no "right" way to heal from Lyme!

I've engaged in both Western and Eastern medicine traditions. I've taken antibiotics and done holistic work. And I believe either can put someone into remission. I've had "good" Herxheimer reactions (again, that's what it's called when Lyme and other toxins die off in your body and cause an overload of symptoms, also known as a Cytokine Storm), and bad ones. I'll get into Herxing in greater depth later, but the "good" Herxes are when you're fully prepared for the symptoms, and when you understand why and what is going on. Having the right mindset, and working with the right doctor when going through a Herx reaction, makes a huge difference. When a doctor did not warn me of any potential side effects when prescribing medication, or didn't give me a clear understanding of what I was getting myself into, it's been really, really tough. In fact, one such experience made me spiral into a deep, dark depression and I thought I was going to die. If you're a Lyme warrior, you'll know that that is not an overstatement. Sometimes, it really does feel like we are dying. So, from my own experience, knowing when I was going to Herx, versus not knowing, has made a huge difference in my mental health during treatment.

As I've said, finding a doctor who listens well and supports you is extremely important. I've been steamrolled by so many doctors, even by Lyme literate doctors. So just because a doctor is highly reputable, and has helped a lot of other people, does not mean he/she/they is the right fit for you! And again: if you find yourself in a situation where it feels like your doctor is not treating *your specific Lyme case*, but rather some generic Lyme template, it's time to move on. Every Lyme warrior is different, and a good doctor will work *with* you to find the best treatment for your body, instead of prescribing the routine set of treatments they use on every patient with Lyme. Of course advocating for yourself can be very hard, especially when it means going against a doctor who claims to have "all the answers." But after a decade of being misdiagnosed, and having people not believe me, I wish I had had the awareness to fight back and demand answers. I know I can't go back in time to change the past, but I *can* help educate others. So it's my hope that if you're reading this, you won't make the same mistakes I did. But the good news is that if your story is similar to mine, it can change! We can always start again. Your health is worth fighting for: again, and again, and again.

Treatment Options

New treatments are popping up all the time, so this list is not all-encompassing, but includes all those I know of that can help treat Lyme disease. And not every Lyme doctor utilizes or specializes in each treatment, which is why it's important to do your own research before choosing a practitioner. But this list can also help you when transitioning to a new treatment or doctor, because there are so many options out there! When you're ready to delve deeper into treatment options, there are many Lyme doctors and specialists who have published books that fully explain every treatment: what it's good for, and why it works. I do recommend working with a doctor and following their particular protocol for your body, at least in the beginning, so you have a clear game plan and don't attempt to tackle this on your own. Likewise, it's important to know that Lyme bacteria do not die easily! They can develop biofilms (a protective shield surrounding the bacteria, which also holds parasites), and there are different forms that the bacteria can take—some of which make them less likely to die. Lyme spirochetes can morph into the cystic form, where they take on a round shape which is often resistant to antibiotic treatments. These "persisters" make eradicating Lyme disease a lot harder, but I'll allow the medical doctors to explain this information to you in greater depth, because they'll do a much better job. Dr. Horowitz's book, *How Can I Get Better?* (St. Martin's/Griffin, 2017), is a good place to start; or Dr. Bill Rawls's *Unlocking Lyme* (FirstDoNoHarm Publishing, 2017). Again: do not try any of the treatments I mention below on your own.

ANTIBIOTICS: There are many different types of antibiotics that doctors use to treat Lyme and its co-infections. They can be taken orally or through an IV. The most common antibiotic I know of is doxycycline. Primary care doctors will prescribe this for acute Lyme, but they often won't prescribe it for long enough (as I noted earlier, the Lyme community feels that people should take an antibiotic for four to six weeks, not two weeks). And for chronic Lyme, I know many people who have taken antibiotics for years. Personally, I'm not a fan of long-term antibiotics, but I do know success stories that have arisen from this method. Again, everyone is different. If you do end up taking lots of antibiotics, make sure to discuss gut health with your doctor, including the importance of taking a highly reputed probiotic.

HYPERTHERMIA: As I described earlier, hyperthermia treatment involves raising your body's temperature—via an injection, or stepping into a special, heated chamber—with the aim of killing Lyme microbes. It can also boost your immune system, disrupt the structural integrity of Lyme bacteria biofilms, and force your body to recognize the Lyme bacteria as a foreign enemy. This treatment is not performed in every state and please note that it's very expensive. Many people travel to Germany or Mexico to get hyperthermia, as they have some of the best-known clinics for this treatment (and the prices can be significantly less abroad).

RIFE MACHINE: Rife machines use electromagnetic frequencies to kill pathogens. This treatment is considered safe for the gut, and does not seem to cause as many Herxheimer reactions as other treatments.

ESSENTIAL OILS: Essential oils have been around since Biblical times. It's important to buy them only from companies that make them safely, because not all brands are equal. DoTERRA and Young Living are two brands I know to be very good. Depending on the oil, you can use it topically, and sometimes even internally, but it's vital to make sure that you do so only while working with a reputable practitioner.

ENERGY HEALING: Our bodies are made up of energy, as is the world. I have found relief engaging in energy healing for the purpose of alleviating food allergies. Energy healing is notably adaptable, as it can be done in person or remotely. Reiki is a well-known variety of energy healing. The practitioner uses palm healing, or hands-on healing, to access a universal energy that is then transferred from them, to the patient. This is meant to encourage emotional and physical healing.

SUPPORTIVE OLIGONUCLEOTIDE TECHNIQUE (SOT) THERAPY: This therapy utilizes short DNA or RNA segments to block the expression of critical genes that Lyme bacteria need to survive and replicate. This is a tailored treatment specifically designed for each individual from blood samples a medical doctor collects and sends off to a specialized lab. SOT therapy is then administered by IV.

BIO RESONANCE: This is another energy-frequency treatment. The practitioner places electrodes on the skin that are hooked up to a machine that reads energy wavelengths in the body. That body energy is then manipulated by the machine with the aim of returning the patient's cell vibrations back to their natural frequency.

HOLISTIC CHIROPRACTORS: This type of chiropractor can not only realign the body, but also the brain. Neurological realignment can be very beneficial for healing chronic illnesses and pain. These professionals will typically assess your overall health as well—something really important for treating Lyme.

HERBAL (& OTHER PLANT) TREATMENT: Using plants, especially herbs, to treat chronic illnesses and diseases is a longtime practice in many cultures. These natural substances often possess potent ingredients that can help treat Lyme disease, co-infections, parasites, and more. There are so many different varieties, but here are some of the most popular ones used by members of the Lyme community: oregano oil, cistus tea, mimosa pudica seed, sida acuta, cats claw, biocidin, grapefruit seed oil, activated charcoal, Japanese knotwood, curcumin, glutathione, berberine, and cryptolepis. You can check out Dr. Rawls's various herbal protocols, The Cowden Protocol (Dr. Lee Cowden's widely known, monthly protocol that rotates 14 NutraMedix herbal products), and Microbe Formulas (Dr. Todd Watts and Dr. Jay Davidson's herbal supplement company) to name a few doctors and companies with great herbal and other plant treatments.

ANTIPARASITICS: Antiparasitic medications are like antibiotics for parasites, and it's said that everyone who's got a heartbeat will have had a parasite at one point or another! More simply, parasites are not nearly as uncommon as people think. In fact Babesia—the common co-infection of Lyme disease I mentioned earlier—makes your body more prone to parasites. Again, this is just one way to treat them. You can check out Dr. Dietrich Klinghardt's well-known parasite protocol (that utilizes multiple antiparasitics).

MAGNET THERAPY: This therapy can also be done in person or remotely. The practitioner uses positive and negative magnets to change the body's susceptibility to certain infections. The pathogen being targeted is then meant to die off, or if still present, its threat will become neutralized.

MIND BODY SPIRIT RELEASE (MBSR): MBSR is an effective energy healing technique developed by Tracy Southwick. It helps release negative emotions, experiences, and trauma trapped inside your body and, in doing so, helps you heal at a holistic level.

DISULFIRAM: This is a type of medication. It has been used to treat alcohol abuse but recently, it's also been shown to help kill Lyme bacteria. Note that it's recommended to get periodic liver tests while taking a course of disulfiram (brand name Antabuse).

BEE VENOM THERAPY: Apitherapy has been around for some 5,000 years. Live bees will sting you on specific points of your body, usually on either side of your spine. Bee venom contains anti-inflammatory properties, certain enzymes, and other active compounds that can help to kill Lyme bacteria, and rid you of other toxins.

SALT THERAPY: This natural remedy involves inhaling pharmaceutical-grade dry salt in a controlled setting. A medical device called a Halogenerator—a machine that grinds down pharmaceutical-grade rock salt—disperses microscopic salt particles into the room, and you'll breathe these tiny particles in for their healing benefits. Salt therapy can help reduce inflammation, absorb impurities, regulate your pH level, and promote your skin's good bacteria.

LIGHT THERAPY: Sitting near a specialized light-therapy box can help with depression, especially seasonal affective disorder (SAD). This light can trigger the release of serotonin (a feel-good chemical) in your brain. Note that it's important to be sure you're purchasing a light box from a well-known outfitter, and that the device is properly certified.

PHAGE THERAPY: Bacteriophages (aka phages) are a form of virus used to treat bacterial infections. This therapy can be employed instead of antibiotics when the bacteria being treated have developed antibiotic resistance. Phages were first independently identified by British bacteriologist Frederick William Twort in 1915, and by French-Canadian microbiologist Félix d'Herelle in 1917, and have been used to treat dysentery, cholera, and gangrene. When antibiotics were made commercially available in the 1930s, doctors lost interest in phages, but recently they've been reintroduced in the fight against certain cancers, as well as Lyme disease.

KAMBO: This healing technique has long been used by Amazonian indigenous people in South America. Shamans will perform a ritual that includes making small burn marks on your skin, and then placing the poisonous-if-ingested secretion of a particular tropical frog where those burn blisters develop. The treatment induces a fever-like state, which is said to help fight off infections as it induces intense vomiting. This process is meant to help purge the body of toxins.

CAVITATION SURGERY: Dental cavitation surgery, conducted by an oral surgeon, is sought out by those with infected gum tissue. Many people with Lyme find that the bacteria can live in places like a wisdom tooth's cavitation. Once the affected areas are addressed, some find their condition improved. Finding a holistic/biological dentist can make a huge difference for people with Lyme.

BRAIN REWIRING: The human brain has the ability to rewire or restructure itself, a process referred to as neuroplasticity. Some with chronic illnesses find brain rewiring to be monumental in their healing journeys. Our brains are extremely powerful, but they can get stuck in patterns of negative thinking. It's important to note that if this happens, it's not your fault. The limbic system controls the brain's emotional and behavioral responses, and when this gets disturbed from trauma (such as Lyme disease), we can get stuck in survival mode (often called "fight or flight mode"). Rewiring this system can help shift our brains into a parasympathetic state—one of growth and repair, where healing can happen more easily. Many people have healed their food allergies, chemical sensitives, chronic pain, and more by utilizing this therapy. The most common programs are Annie Hopper's Dynamic Neural Retraining System (DNRS), and Ashok Gupta's Gupta Program Brain Retraining, but there are tons of other coaches and programs out there as well.

OZONE THERAPY: Medical ozone can be administered intravenously, taken orally, and can be inserted into the colon. This integrative treatment increases the amount of oxygen in the body. Intravenous ozone involves drawing blood from the patient, exposing it to ozone (which is meant to "clean" the blood), and then re-injecting it back into the vein. The main purpose of this treatment is to detox the body, suppress infection, and boost the immune system. Many people feel a huge shift in their energy levels after this treatment.

HYPERBARIC OXYGEN CHAMBER: This is another treatment that aims to increase oxygen levels in the body. The patient lies down in a specialized chamber where they breathe in pressurized oxygen. The air pressure is increased to two or three times the normal air pressure in order to increase the amount of oxygen in the blood. As the newly boosted blood circulates through your body, it's meant to help fight bacteria and promote healing.

STEM CELL THERAPY: Innovative stem cell treatments can have potent anti-inflammatory effects. When received via IV, the stem cells travel throughout the body, seeking out inflammation and damaged tissues. Stem cell therapy can be very expensive, but the anti-inflammatory effects have been known to last for years.

GROUNDING: Also known as "earthing," this therapy is meant to allow you to make direct contact with the earth's energy field. Often, one does this by standing barefoot on the ground. This process is meant to provide feelings of mental and physical well-being, and what's great about this treatment is that it's free.

DETOXIFICATION: As explained earlier, detox treatments remove toxins from the body. This typically includes drainage systems, as making sure your systems are open and moving is crucial in the fight against Lyme disease. This means pooping and sweating every day in an effort to kill toxins, and making sure they actually leave your body! Detox treatments include lymphatic massage (a massage treatment that encourages the movement of lymph fluids around the body, as making sure one's lymphatic system is open and moving is important), ionic foot baths (a foot soak that uses water charged with positive and negative ions to help pull toxins out of the body, through the feet), infrared saunas (a sauna that penetrates more deeply beneath the skin), Epsom salt baths (a natural occurring mineral salt made up of magnesium and sulfate meant to soothe muscles and inflammation when used in the bath), apple cider vinegar (ACV) baths (ACV has powerful antimicrobials properties), castor oil liver packs (a piece of wool or cloth soaked in castor oil and placed above the liver with a heating pad on top), coffee enemas (a type of colon cleanse using a detoxifying mix of coffee and water), and colonics (a type of colon cleanse that flushes out large portions of the bowel system), just to name a few. (Note that Epsom salt baths are safe, but because I had what my care team believes was extreme mold toxicity, and skin inflammation from COVID-19, my body "wept" out black gunk. This shouldn't happen to you.)

SUPPLEMENTS: Dietary supplements are designed to provide certain nutrients, and to help organ function. Supplements come in pill, liquid, or powder form, and can significantly aid in the healing journey. This said, supplements are not FDA regulated so it's important to purchase them from a reputable distributor. Also, they often need to be taken at certain times of the day, and either with or without food. Be sure to consult with your physician before starting supplements, and to follow packaging directions carefully.

BINDERS: Supplements that help bind toxins together in your body, thereby reducing their harmful effects, are known as "binders." They are particularly important to take when trying to kill Lyme bacteria, as they can help lessen Herxheimer reactions. Some common binders include activated charcoal, bentonite clay, and chlorella, but there are many more! Again, be sure to consult your doctor before starting, and to follow packaging directions closely. Note that some binders need to be taken two hours before or after taking other foods and medications, so be sure to plan ahead.

ACUPUNCTURE: This ancient Chinese medical treatment involves inserting thin needles into specific parts of the body to promote healing. Acupuncture can help reduce inflammation, pain, anxiety, brain fog, fatigue, and much more. There are even some acupuncturists who specialize in the treatment of Lyme disease.

INTRAVENOUS IMMUNOGLOBULIN THERAPY (IVIG): IVIG fluid contains antibodies that your body is not making on its own, and it is administered intravenously. The treatment can help fight off infections and raise low red-blood-cell counts.

DESERET BIOLOGICALS SERIES THERAPY (DesBio): An immunological treatment that works with the body to develop a targeted approach to killing and controlling infections. This homeopathic treatment helps your immune system recognize Lyme, and other co-infections, as foreign invaders and start to attack them.

Cost-Effective Treatments You Can Do Yourself!

Lyme treatments are often astronomically expensive, and insurance typically covers very little. Things need to change but, for now, here are a few free, or cost-effective treatments you can try if finances are an issue. I want to be clear that I think it's imperative that you work with a doctor, practitioner, or healer of some sort, but if you can't at the present moment, or are in between medical teams, this chapter explains treatment methodologies you can do on your own. Everybody is different, so try things out, and change it up if something's not helping.

CHANGE YOUR DIET: Inflammation is a huge issue in chronic Lyme disease, and lowering it is key. Luckily, changing your diet is a cost-effective way to help you in this pursuit. Before I was diagnosed, I cut out gluten, dairy, and eventually sugar because I found that it made me feel better. My food allergy tests all came back negative, and doctors told me that I didn't have Celiac disease, but I still feel improved by not eating gluten, and that's all that matters. Many people swear by the low-inflammatory keto(genic), and Paleo(lithic) diets. Some also go vegan. I suggest trying different diets out, to see what works for you. Another option is intermittent fasting, which can be a great way to realign your gut. Indeed various types of short and long fasting can also be beneficial. This said: before you begin any kind of dietary change or consider any kind of fast, it's really important to first consult with a doctor. Also note that your diet need not change forever. Allergies are not always lifelong, especially in Lyme patients. For instance, if you've all of a sudden developed a dairy allergy, you may actually have a parasite, so treating the root cause may alleviate the problem.

DETOX: I spoke about detox treatments in the prior section, but they're worth mentioning again here because there are many ways to detox that are cost effective—as well as extremely important for healing! Taking detox baths with either Epsom salt or apple cider vinegar (I've used both at the same time!) cost very little, and you can find both at your local convenience store. I have a personal, infrared sauna I use a few times a week that was less than $200 on Amazon. This sauna has saved me an enormous amount of money because a single sauna session at a gym or a spa can be expensive. Castor oil packs are also a great way to detox your liver for under $50. They're good for multiple conditions, and often last several months. All you need is wool flannel, castor oil, and a heating pad (I like to take a spoonful of olive oil before or after to help aid in flushing out the liver, gallbladder, and biliary tract).

CUT OUT STRESS: One way to de-stress is to surround yourself with people who love you. Another is leaving the haters behind. People can be toxic, and negative relationships affect your health more than you might realize.

SELF-CARE: Practice self-care every day. This can include meditation, watching your favorite TV shows, doing yoga, etc. Do anything that makes you feel happy, calm, and rejuvenated.

REST: Your body is fighting hard for you, day in and day out. So sometimes, the best thing we can do to help ourselves heal is to rest. Resting is not doing nothing! It's making an active choice to help your own healing. I encourage you to listen to your body and rest as often as you can. This also includes getting a full night's sleep, which is super important because our bodies get rejuvenated as we sleep.

MOVE YOUR BODY: Don't fall into the trap of *only* resting, because movement is just as important. We have to get oxygen to our organs, get that lymphatic system pumping, and get our circulatory system working. If you can't go for a walk or do yoga, simple stretches from your bed can go a long way.

LAUGHTER: Laughing is scientifically proven to boost your mood, reduce pain, and stimulate oxygen to your organs. People think I'm crazy when I mention how much laughter has helped me, but it's true. It's one of the best tools I've found in my healing journey, and it's free! Also, your body can't tell the difference between fake laughter and real laughter, so if you've heard the phrase "fake it till you make it," try "fake laughing" at least once a day. You might be pleasantly surprised when your mood shifts, and soon enough, you're very likely to start finding humor all around you!

BRAIN RETRAINING/REWIRING: As I mentioned before, there are programs like Annie Hopper's Dynamic Neural Retraining System (DNRS), and Ashok Gupta's Gupta Program Brain Retraining, that typically cost several hundred dollars, but you can also find free workshops and cheap books to get you started. Dr. Joe Dispenza has some great books and YouTube videos! Getting in a positive mindset is also beneficial. As best you can, stop focusing on your symptoms and start focusing on things that bring you joy. Visualize your healthy future, meditate on healing, and know that it is possible!

EDUCATE YOURSELF: Learn about Lyme disease, and your specific symptoms. Read articles online and buy books—or borrow them from the library—to learn as much as you can. We have to be the boss of our healing, and the more you can educate yourself about what's going on in your body, the better equipped you'll be to head into battle. This can also help you decide which treatments are best for you.

BE IN NATURE: Get outside as often as you're able. Soak up that free Vitamin D from the sun, breathe in fresh air, and surround yourself with the healing properties of nature. Vitamin D deficiencies are actually very common in those with Lyme. And as I mentioned before, "grounding" is a great and cost-free technique to connect ourselves with the earth. Personally, I find the beach to be extremely healing. If you're near a beach, try to stick your feet in the ocean, watch the sunset, and listen to the birds. Of course, it's important to protect yourself against ticks and to conduct tick checks when and after you're outside, but don't be afraid of getting back into nature! We have to change up the monotony of our routines at home, and if you're bedbound, try to sit by an open window. Do whatever you can to receive the gifts of nature, because they really are so healing.

Toxin Overload: Co-Infections, Mold, Parasites, Heavy Metals, & Electric and Magnetic Fields (EMFs)

Ticks carry more than just Lyme disease (Borrelia bacteria). They also carry a plethora of other infections. Many people do not realize that these other co-infections could be the reason that they're as sick as they are, or why they have not yet gotten better. These co-infections can and often include Babesia, which I've mentioned several times, as well as Bartonella (the bacteria that causes "Cat Scratch Disease," an infection of the lymph nodes following a scratch or bite from a cat), Ehrlichia (a group of at least three bacterial sub-species that cause disease), Rickettsia (the bacteria that causes Rocky Mountain Spotted Fever), Anaplasma (a bacteria causing Anaplasmosis disease), and Mycoplasma (a stealth pathogen that can cause respiratory infections and other diseases). Other reasons people don't get better include mold, parasites, heavy metals, and EMFs. When someone has chronic Lyme disease, it's usually because their body has a toxin overload. This overload is often the reason Lyme has become activated, and why people get so sick. Yes, some people can get Lyme disease and stay healthy. Finding this out was challenging for me, because it doesn't seem fair. But here's the thing, my symptoms were dormant for a decade before my toxin overload got activated, back when I got a parasite in Guatemala. So, if people stay healthy and aren't exposed to other toxins, then they might be fine. Then again, they might not. I recommend that everyone who gets bitten by a tick seeks treatment at once. But this chapter is for *you* right now, someone who's already battling chronic Lyme and needs to know why it can be so challenging to get better.

There are tests for co-infections, mold, parasites, heavy metals, and EMF (more about those shortly) exposure. But just like the tests for Lyme disease, these are not always accurate. Especially when it comes to parasite testing! I can't tell you how many times I've pooped in a cup, sent it off to a lab to look for parasites, and had it come back negative. And yet I have them! A lot of them. If you have chronic Lyme, you most likely have some of these issues, whether you test positive for them or not. But again, every Lyme warrior is different, and I can't possibly know your story, nor do I want to generalize Lyme patient stories. Still, here are some other issues to test and treat for in order to help make all this a little easier.

Test for toxins and co-infections with a reputable lab, and track your symptoms to see if they match up with any other infections. For instance, night sweats are linked to Babesia. A lot of these conditions' symptoms overlap, but each of them also have distinct symptoms you can look out for. Here are some common symptoms of a few tick-borne infections. For more in-depth information, I recommend checking out Dr. Rawls' diagrams (available at Rawlsmd.com).

BABESIA:

- Chest or rib pain

- Drenching night sweats

- Body temperature fluctuations

- Air hunger (a feeling of severe breathlessness)

- Dark-colored urine

- Abdominal pain

- Red moles on skin

BARTONELLA:

- Rage episodes

- Mental health issues

- Blurred vision

- Dry or red eyes

- Ringing in the ears

- Swollen lymph nodes

- Unexplained cough

- Stretch marks

- Skin & bone pain

- Foot pain, particularly in the morning

BORRELIA:

- Stiff neck

- Lyme carditis (when Lyme enters the tissues of the heart)

- Eye floaters

- Bull's-eye rash

- Bell's palsy

- Migrating arthritis

- Joint swelling

MYCOPLASMA

- Respiratory infection
- Sinus problems

Mold is another huge issue for Lyme warriors, and isn't always talked about. Living in a moldy environment could be the reason you're not able to get better. Twenty-five percent of the population has a genetic pre-disposition that makes them more susceptible to mold toxicity and Chronic Inflammatory Response Syndrome (CIRS). But whether you have that pre-disposition or not, mold is another toxin that can overload your system. Many Lyme warriors will immediately feel the effects of mold in their system if they enter a moldy location. It can feel like, all of a sudden, you have a terrible cold; or the flu; and the exposure can cause a Lyme flare. It doesn't happen so drastically for everyone, but I do recommend testing your living environment for mold just to make sure. Some people will leave a moldy environment, and notice an immediate difference in their health! You can test your home with the Environmental Relative Moldiness Index (ERMI) test, or hire a certified mold inspector—just make sure they're familiar with Lyme disease, because standard mold inspectors won't realize that even the smallest amount of mold can affect us. You can also test yourself for mold toxins with a specific urine test. Most Lyme doctors know this test, and prescribe it. But some doctors don't believe mold is as big of an issue as it can be, so if you think you're dealing with mold, I encourage you to keep searching for answers, and to keep seeking treatment.

Parasites are ruthless, and the truth is, they're very common. It's wrong to think that parasites are only in third-world countries, because they're everywhere, and whether you deal with a chronic illness or not, you've encountered parasites. Sure, you can't always see them, but that doesn't mean they aren't there. Many parasites are microscopic, though the ones you can see are usually inside your poop. It might sound gross, but when parasite cleansing, if you dissect your poop (with a plastic utensil of some sort) you might be shocked at what you find! There are a few key things I want to note about parasites, that I really wish I had known before starting Lyme treatments. First, as I've mentioned several times: I wish I had sought treatment for parasites before undergoing hyperthermia because they carry Lyme disease and other toxins, so if you don't address them first, Lyme will continue to live in your body, inside of them. Second, if you have the co-infection Babesia, Dr. Horowitz states that it can suppress your immune system's ability to eliminate other parasites. Third, as I've also already noted, stool tests for parasites are highly inaccurate. Most of my friends who have Lyme and parasites were never able to get a positive parasite test, myself included. As I said before, I've literally taken worms that I've passed to a lab for testing, scared all of the technicians working that day, and the results still came back negative. Fourth, parasites can be really hard to kill. Most people assume you can take an antiparasitic and be done with them, but it's the same story as for Lyme disease—a simple dose of antibiotics rarely works (at least for someone who's dealing with multiple toxins). Fifth, parasites cause GI upset, and are nocturnal. So, if you find yourself dealing with strange bloating, gas, constipation, nausea, sugar cravings, and insomnia, you might have parasites to "thank." Sixth, there are many different types of parasites, and they all respond to different treatments.

Liver flukes are a big issue for many people who have Lyme, and they don't look like worms. They often look like little slugs, tomato skins, or corn kernels, and they clog sufferers' livers. So, if you find yourself having a hard time detoxing your liver, it might be clogged with flukes. All in all, even if you don't see any parasites when you go to the bathroom, you still might have them.

Heavy metals are another toxin that can overload many people with chronic Lyme. And just the way parasites can hold onto Lyme, they can also hold onto heavy metals. We all encounter heavy metals because, sadly, our world is very toxic. People spray poisonous chemicals on the foods we eat, and put them in the beauty products we use. The most common metals that get trapped in our bodies are lead, mercury, arsenic, and aluminum. They can cause developmental disorders, autoimmune conditions, neurological problems, and even cancer. There are urine and blood tests that your doctor can prescribe to see if you battle heavy metals, and there are treatments that can help! Chelation, a treatment that uses special medicine to bind to metals in your blood, is the main intravenous detox treatment I know of, but there are also many things you can do yourself, from the comfort of your home. Just as with Lyme, you need to get your lymphatic system flowing to help flush out heavy metals. Some easy ways to do this include: 1) Consuming organic produce to reduce pesticides and herbicide contamination. 2) Eating alkalizing vegetables to help balance your pH, and the acid level in your body. 3) Adding cilantro, parsley, and dandelion to your diet because they are naturally detoxing herbs. 4) Detoxifying your body by dry brushing, and by using an infrared sauna, or bath. 5) Drinking a lot of water to push everything through! Hydrating is so important. But make sure your water is filtered, spring, or distilled (everyone has an opinion of which water to drink, so do what's best for you—but avoid tap or unfiltered water).

Electric and magnetic fields can be another big issue for people who battle chronic Lyme disease. These are invisible energy waves from our cell phones, computers, powerlines, Wi-Fi routers, microwaves, etc. They send radiation into our bodies. Some people don't seem to have a problem with this exposure, some don't believe it exists, and others can't be near any EMFs at all. There are studies showing the link between EMFs and cancer, but that won't stop companies from continuing to produce faster and more "efficient" products like 5G. Personally, I haven't felt the debilitating effects that I know EMFs can cause for some. But that's not to say I'm not being exposed. Technology is still so new in the grand scheme of life on Earth, that I really don't think anyone knows how it might affect the human population in years to come. Cell phones and the internet are incredible technological advances that have also greatly impacted our world for good! Do we "need" these things? Frankly, in today's day and age, yes we do. Would our world be a healthier place without them? Most definitely. We can't change the world, but we can change the way we live in it. As I said before, I'm grateful that I really don't feel a difference in my body (that I know of) from my own EMF exposure, but I try to limit it when I can. Little things like not standing in front of the microwave, using your cellphone on speaker mode so you're not holding it directly against your ear, and keeping cell phones and computers away from your bed when you sleep at night, are a few changes you can make to help reduce your own exposure.

Order of Operations: What Do You Treat First?

There is no "right way" to treat Lyme disease, co-infections, and other toxins in the body. Many people and many doctors will tell you that there is. Now, that's their opinion, which they're entitled to, but I've seen friends reach remission by doing all sorts of different treatments in all different orders. That being said, this is my book and I'm going to express my opinion about what I believe to be the best order of operations, which is: **1) drainage 2) parasites 3) heavy metals and mold 4) Lyme and co-infections and 5) viruses and chemicals**.

Drainage (how your body removes toxins) has to be addressed first and foremost because, if your pathways aren't open, there's no place for the toxins to go when you kill them, and that can cause serious Herxheimer reactions, and other issues. Opening your drainage pathways means addressing your lymphatic system and GI systems, to make sure you are sweating and pooping every day. When you're treating parasites, many people say you should be pooping at least twice a day. If you're not doing that, there are supplements you can take to move your bowels along, or you can do enemas. Some ways to aid in drainage are lymphatic massages, rebounding (jumping on small trampolines), detoxifying IV treatments, vibration plates (an electric device you stand on that provides multidirectional vibrations to calm the nervous system and drain the lymphatic system), castor oil packs, infrared saunas, ionic foot baths, coffee enemas, and more. Certain supplements can address drainage as well, and opening up these pathways can take a few months. Don't be alarmed if your doctor wants you to focus only on your drainage systems before you start killing anything. It's important to do so.

I think it's important to address parasites next. As I've said, I didn't do this when I first started my Lyme journey, and I wish I did. Most everyone gets parasites, and they become a huge issue for many Lyme warriors. I've told you that testing is terrible, and that every stool test I completed came back negative—even when I took the worms directly to the lab. But, if you find yourself with Candida (yeast); IBS, SIBO, or other gut issues; you most likely have parasites. So, if you don't treat them first, you can't truly eradicate Lyme disease. I've seen a lot of people heal from Lyme, but then have it come back because they never addressed parasites. This was my story too, so now I'm working hard to kill these suckers. As I mentioned earlier, I've been passing massive tapeworms lately! It takes months or even years to eradicate parasites but, given how far I've come, I'm living proof that it can be done. (It's also worth mentioning that some people find they don't need to continue other treatments once parasites are gone. Most, if not all, of my Lyme symptoms have diminished after parasite cleansing. Everyone is different, but this has been my experience in how beneficial getting rid of parasites can be.)

Next it's time to treat for heavy metals and mold. Once the parasites are gone, you can finally start addressing the toxins that they were once carrying. Some people jump right to Lyme disease, or even treat heavy metals, mold, and Lyme nearly simultaneously. I'm taking binders (again, specific supplements that help bind toxins together in your body, reducing their harmful effects) along with parasite-killing herbs, and this is aiding in the removal of my mold and heavy metals. My levels of each are not extremely high but, I did have mold leak out of my skin, which

I'm happy to note has not happened again since treating parasites. As I mentioned earlier, chelation is also really useful for heavy metal detoxification. That, and taking binders, and then sweating it out—like hopping in an infrared sauna—helps to pull these toxins out of your body. Again, sweating and pooping are the two main ways that we release toxins.

After you've opened up your drainage pathways, treated your parasites, heavy metals and mold, now you can treat Lyme disease and co-infections. I mentioned many treatment options earlier, ones that can help eradicate these infections. So, once parasites are gone, and your toxin level is significantly decreased, I think you have a better chance of truly eradicating Lyme. And since parasites carry the Lyme bacteria, and you've worked hard to kill those worms, you might find that your Lyme levels and symptoms have lessened in comparison to when you first tested.

Finally, after you've treated Lyme and co-infections, many people go on to address viruses and chemicals. One common virus Lyme warriors deal with is Epstein-Barr. When you're dealing with a compromised immune system, your body has a hard time fighting off anything, so many Lyme warriors also deal with viruses and chemical toxicity. Like heavy metals and mold, there are certain binders and detox protocols that can address these issues. I've recently learned that my filtered water carries a plethora of environmental toxins that are feeding my parasites, so next on my list is to address these toxins and chemicals with binders, alongside more parasite treatments. So, although I write this order of operations as separate steps, many people combine certain treatments and need to jump back and forth between these steps as they heal. There is no "correct" way to treat Lyme disease. We learn as we go, and we must keep going.

All this said, it's important to follow your doctor's protocol, but again: if he/she/they are treating Lyme disease in a different order, I urge you to ask them why, and see if they'd be open to a different plan of attack. Not everyone will be, and some probably find great success in their own order of operations. Every doctor is different, and every patient's body is unique and will respond differently to treatments. Also, not everyone deals with all of the toxins I mentioned above. But looking back at my own journey, and learning just how many people are infected with toxins but don't realize it, I hope you'll consider my recommendations before you make any final preparations for treating Lyme disease. I wish I had, and since this book is meant to include all my failures and realizations, I knew it was important to add this chapter.

Different Approaches to Killing Lyme: Kill, Kill, Kill vs. Support

Everyone, everywhere, has a different opinion about how to treat and effectively kill Lyme disease. I'll continue to repeat that there is no "correct" way to go about it. That's why it's really important that you find a doctor you trust who listens to you, and supports what you want to do. If you don't know what you want to do, that's okay, too. We all have to start somewhere, and being under the guidance of a good doctor is the perfect place to start. Both Eastern and Western approaches can, and do, work. What I've noticed though, is that the philosophies behind these approaches can be vastly different. That is, some will want to "kill, kill, kill," and some will want to focus on supporting your body. Yes,

63

some will want to both "support and kill," and others will want only to support your immune system, to allow your body to do what it does best: protect you. I do believe the human body is an incredible force of nature, and that we all have the power within us to heal. But I also believe that many, if not most of us, need some help along the way.

The doctors who use the "kill, kill, kill" approach usually suggest more aggressive treatments, such as multiple antibiotics at once in order to target and kill as much Lyme bacteria, and as many co-infections, as possible. I've found a lot of MDs and LLMDs go about it this way. And this approach can and does work! I've had many friends go through six months to a year of intense killing treatments and now, they've never felt better. I've also had friends take years and years of multiple antibiotics at once, had their hair fall out, and not get any better. There's no way to know until you try. But I suggest that if you tap into your intuition, you'll naturally be able to determine the approach that's best for you. Generally, and not always, I've found the more aggressive approach produces more significant Herxheimer reactions—to be discussed at length in the next chapter—than the slower, supporting approach.

The doctors who take the "support" approach are often holistic doctors, naturopaths, and other types of healers. Many MDs use this approach, too. I can't and don't mean to generalize, but my own experience and research has shown me that holistic doctors are quicker to support our bodies and use a less aggressive approach when it comes to the "killing." These supportive treatments, such as herbs, can still cause Herxheimer reactions. But usually, the body is more equipped to handle them because it's being supported along the way.

You'll want to consider your specific tolerance levels as well.

Personally, I'm extremely sensitive to medications, and antibiotics were not the right treatment for me. I tried the "kill, kill, kill" method, and it was too intense. But that's how my body works, which won't necessarily be how yours does. I just want to point out these two vastly different approaches when it comes to Lyme treatments, because I was unaware of them when I first started my healing journey. I also want to note that other Lyme warriors, as well as friends who happened to know someone with Lyme, sometimes had *very* strong opinions about how they thought I should heal, what treatment I should do next, etc. Their advice usually came from a place of love, but if acquaintances, or friends or family members, suggest a treatment plan that doesn't resonate with you, it's okay for you to say, no! I encourage you to stay your course, pivot when needed (more on this later), but don't make any rash decisions about your own journey just because someone made you feel like you weren't treating Lyme "correctly." There is no right or wrong—there's only healing—and I can promise you it's not linear.

Herxheimer Reactions

Jarisch Herxheimer reactions (JHR), usually referred to in this book as a Herx, Herx reaction, or Herxing, are bodily detoxification reactions that result from killing off harmful bacteria and other toxins—especially when Lyme spirochetes die. Many antibiotics will cause you to Herx, as will certain holistic treatments. I was not aware of just how debilitating Herx reactions could be, and I wish I had read a chapter like this before starting my treatments. Lyme itself can cross the blood brain barrier and create mental health issues—even more so when the bacteria die off.

Herxheimer reactions are brutal, both mentally and physically, but again: I was not prepared for them. I'm not sure which was worse, the pain or the mental breakdowns, but everyone is different, and so each person's bacterial die off will therefore be different, too. It's not easy, but you aren't alone! Here are some tips to get you through some of the worst Herxheimer reactions:

1. Mentally prepare as best you can. Herxing usually happens within a few hours after your treatment. But that time frame is not exact. They can occur earlier, or much later, too. Know that Herxheimer reactions can very often cause depression and/or anxiety. If you start to feel different, name it; and be ready to call your support system (family, friends, support groups, etc.) to ask for help. When I Herxed, I would go from zero to 100 with either extreme depression (i.e., all of a sudden I would feel like my life didn't matter), or extreme anxiety (i.e., bordering on a panic attack, and feeling like I was going to die). These are normal feelings that can occur when you're experiencing a die off, and recognizing them will help you stay grounded. Realizing, "it's the toxins!" and not *you* is really important.

2. Bind! Take extra binders to soak up all of the bad toxins floating around in your body. I love activated charcoal, and CellCore's BioToxin Binder, but there are tons of binders out there that can help with die off. But again, it's important to seek a professional's input before you go on a buying spree—especially if you take other medications.

3. Detox! Hop in an infrared sauna or Epsom salt bath, and sweat out all the bad stuff—but make sure your pathways are open (meaning you're pooping and sweating regularly, with no issues), and that your lymphatic system is working well (as mentioned before this can take weeks to months of focusing solely on detoxing). Ideally, you want to make sure you're having bowel movements every day. If you aren't pooping daily, there are supplements your doctor can prescribe for you, and you can talk about doing coffee (or water) enemas. I can assure you that once you start killing bacteria and releasing toxins, you'll want them to leave your body as soon as possible! The quicker they exit, the fewer symptoms you'll experience. So, this is why I highly recommend making detoxing a priority before, during, and after treatments.

4. Stay positive. Keep telling yourself that "this will pass" and "this won't last forever." It's also okay to just cry it out! Sometimes we need to have that emotional purge in order to feel better and have some release. It's important to feel everything you're feeling, but not to ruminate on it. Getting in the mindset that "everything will be okay," will help you better prepare for any and all Herx reactions. Remember: this truly is part of the healing journey, and you are such a warrior for going through it!

5. Rest and engage in self-care. Give yourself extra love during this time, and take it easy. Put on your favorite TV show or movie (preferably a comedy, to boost some of that feel-good serotonin in your brain), snuggle up in cozy blankets, find a heating pad, and relax. Your body is fighting so hard for you; the best thing you can do for it is to stay calm, and take it easy.

I also want to note that Herxing doesn't get any easier as you go through this journey but having a plan, and developing your own kind of "tool kit," can make a huge difference. Just know that everything you're feeling is valid and "normal," in the sense that killing off Lyme bacteria sometimes just sucks. Some doctors and patients encourage Herxheimer reactions, while others try to avoid them completely. I don't know anyone who truly enjoys Herxing, but certain treatments—and the pace of your treatments—can really determine whether you'll Herx or not. This is very important to bring up with your doctor so you can come up with a plan that works best for you. Also, sometimes we Herx without meaning to, because our bodies are fighting so hard for us that they decide to kill things off on their own. And just because you Herxed during a treatment the last time, does not necessarily mean you'll Herx during it again! Reactions vary, and can come and go, but knowing how to spot the signs of a Herx can help you prepare for the fight ahead. You've got this, and I'm rooting for you!

A Treatment Didn't Work: When to Pivot

This happens. Not every treatment works, and not every doctor gets it right the first time. It sucks, but's it's life, and there are a few things I want to say about it. First, this is, unfortunately, a very normal part of the healing process; and second, no it was not a waste of your time and money. It's normal because everyone's different and there is no magic pill that cures Lyme disease or its co-infections. After assessing your symptoms and lab results, every doctor makes their best educated guess on how to proceed. As patients, we must start somewhere, but trying new treatments is incredibly important. And you should be proud of yourself for putting yourself out there, because I am proud of you! It's important to not live in the mindset that a treatment that didn't work was a "waste." The treatment you went through, whatever it was, most likely did kill Lyme bacteria. It also showed you what didn't work so you can reassess your plan and come up with a different mode of attack. Most likely, it also showed you just how strong you are. If you didn't realize it before, Lyme warriors are some of the strongest people on this planet.

So you're no longer angry with your doctor for "failing you," and you aren't crying about it being a "waste," so what next? Well, first you need to have an honest conversation with yourself and/or your caregiver about how you feel about your doctor. Here are a few questions you can ask to see whether it's time to find a new one or not:

- •- How do I feel walking into and out of my doctor's office?

- • Can I be honest and truthful with my doctor about every symptom I've been having?

- • Does my doctor listen to me and validate my experience and concerns when I have an appointment?

- • Has my doctor been there for me emotionally during scary Herxheimer reactions?

- • Has my doctor walked me through my treatments, and why I'm undergoing them?

- • Does my doctor have a new treatment in mind, since this one didn't work? What is it, and why will it be different?

• Does my doctor treat me like an *individual* who has Lyme, or like a generic Lyme patient?

• Do I think this doctor will help me reach remission?

Once you can answer these questions, you'll have a better sense about whether or not you should stay with your doctor. Many practitioners will have multiple plans of attack for Lyme patients, but some will only have one. If your doctor is a one-plan kind of person, and you already tried it and it didn't work, then it's clearly time to move on.

If you've decided to stay, that's great too. Only you, and you alone, will know whether someone's a good fit or not, and it's okay if this changes over time. It's so important to find a doctor you trust, and who believes in you. If you've found him/her/them, then I'm so happy for you. If you've decided to move on, that's okay too! It happens. I've left many doctors when I felt like things weren't progressing, and there is no shame in moving on. You WILL find the practitioner who's the best fit for you! But it can be daunting, I know. So here are some steps you can take to find your next doctor and treatment, if you've decided to move on:

1. Reach out to the Lyme community for referrals again. The best referrals are from people you already know and trust. And at this point, you've probably been treating Lyme for a few months, or a few years, and have a better understanding of the doctors out there.

2. Research treatments again, so this time you can be more

specific about what you want. Listen to podcasts and other social media outlets that interview Lyme patients about which doctors they've seen and which treatments they've done. Some other groups, advocates, and doctors I enjoy listening to are Lyme 360, The Tick Chicks, Dahl Holistic Health, Lyme and Cancer Services, and San Diego Lyme Alliance. I also want to note that Dr. Klinghardt, Dr. Rawls, and Dr. Marty Ross often host free webinars with a Q & A portion!

3. If you can't find anyone locally, many doctors do telemedicine! Don't let location stop you from seeking out the best. I've worked remotely with many doctors, and had great success with it.

4. Think about your worst symptom and make a list of the doctors who specialize in that area. For me, it's been those from parasites. But please note that just because a doctor might be a world-renowned specialist, that doesn't mean he/she/they will be the right doctor for you.

5. Be open to holistic doctors as well as traditional doctors. Sometimes the best doctors and treatments are not who and what you thought would help you heal. Energy healing and non-traditional medicine has been a game changer for me!

Be the Boss of Your Healing

It took me years to understand this concept, and it's okay if it feels out of reach for you right now but, at the end of the day, you must be your own boss when it comes to healing. You are in charge of what you do, who you see, and when to change something up. As I've said before: your doctors work for YOU, not the other way around. If you want to get a specific blood test, your doctor should be able to prescribe it for you, and you certainly shouldn't fear asking. Only you are going to know how you feel during a treatment. Your doctor can make an educated guess, and help to prepare you for Herxheimer reactions, but they will not know how you're truly feeling. So, if something intuitively feels off, speak up! As I said before, treatments will either work with your body or against your body, and only you will be able to tell the difference.

What makes someone a boss? Think about the most successful people you know. What are some things that make them stand out? Is it their confidence? Their intelligence? Their drive to be the best? There are varying types of success, but I think every boss has a "tool kit" that makes them successful in their field. So, here are a few things that you can do in order to be the "boss of your own healing":

1. Educate yourself. I've said this before, but I'll keep saying it because it's so important! Learn as much as you can about Lyme disease. If you search randomly around the internet you're guaranteed to encounter a lot of misinformation—so be sure to learn from the best. Read books by other Lyme warriors and doctors. And learn about the specific co-infections you may have. Remember, this is your body, and knowing why you feel a certain way, and what's behind it, can only help you to understand more about yourself. Also, stop when you feel burnt out! Sometimes this information can be stressful and scary. I know, I've been shocked by some of the things I've read, and it's okay to take a break, regroup, and come back to it later.

2. Keep track of your symptoms and of all the treatments you get. This'll be easy if you're a Type A personality, but it may seem overwhelming or even pointless to someone who's Type B. Meaning, if you naturally enjoy being organized, you'll like this idea. If you hate following rules and prefer to live in the moment, I encourage you to have someone on your team (a family member or friend) help you stay on top of everything. My mom has a list of all the doctors I saw when my symptoms first started 12 years ago. I don't have that information, and I was far too sick to keep track of anything back then. I'm grateful to have my mom's support and the organizational skills that I sometimes lack!

3. Be open to new possibilities! The best "bosses" are ones who can adapt easily and quickly to change. Let go of how you think you're going to heal. As I have said repeatedly: I can assure you it probably won't go how you think it's going to go. I encourage you to be open to all kinds of treatments. And remember that healing is mental, physical, and even spiritual. I had a lot of judgement around energy healing when I first started treatments, and I can honestly say that energy healing and holistic treatments and herbs have helped me the most.

4. Don't be afraid to ask for help when you need it. Even the most successful people need guidance, comfort, and help, now and again. When you're dealing with an illness like Lyme disease, you're going to need it, often. So now is the time to put away any pride, or thoughts that you'll need to go at it alone. If you live on your own (like I did) you might physically be alone, but I can assure you, you are not. Lean on your close friends and family. You are NOT a burden. And if you don't feel like you have that kind of support system in place, lean into Lyme support groups. There are many people online willing and able to be there for you. If you don't ask for help, no one will know that you need it. I know it's hard to do—I hate asking for help—but it's really important.

5. Last but not least, trust your gut. Meaning, trust that deep feeling you get when you somehow just "know" whether something is good or bad. Really try to tap into that intuition, because we all have it. If you don't believe that you have it, that's okay, you'll find it when you're ready. But keep listening for it, because I believe our bodies are communicating with us every day.

Part Three: Navigating Day-to-Day Life with Lyme

This next section covers how to *live* while battling Lyme disease: mindset, support communities, work, dating, self-love, and more. People talk a lot about life after Lyme. Well, I'm here to tell you there's life *during* Lyme as well. May these day-to-day tips help you thrive during your healing journey.

You Are Not Your Lyme Diagnosis

After getting a diagnosis, I fell into the trap of centering my identity around Lyme disease. It started to define who I was, and I really enjoyed that initially—for a few reasons—and it's okay if you feel this way too, at first.

I enjoyed it because after years of being misdiagnosed, I finally knew what was wrong, and could give people an answer when they asked me why I was so sick. Second, I enjoyed it because I found a community of people who knew exactly what I was going through. Finally, after years of isolation and hiding my pain, it felt like I fit in somewhere. These are valid feelings! Honestly, I still have these feelings to an extent, but I've redirected my thoughts so that Lyme is no longer my identity—and doing that is crucial for healing.

You are more than Lyme disease, and it's important you know that because you ARE going to heal, and you'll no longer be able to fall back on that diagnosis to define yourself. That's the goal, right? So, think about it: If you're only defining yourself as a person with Lyme disease, how can you possibly heal? Our bodies and minds are used to feeling sick. That's what feels safe and "right," in a sense, but we have to change that narrative. It's not easy to let go of the diagnosis. Trust me, I get it! But you can still be part of the Lyme community, share your diagnosis, and not let it define you. Here are some new identities you can embrace after being diagnosed with Lyme disease:

- **You are a WARRIOR.** You face every battle head on, and I'm proud of you.

- **You are a FIGHTER.** You fight for your life, every single day. Many won't see this fight, but I know it well, and encourage you to keep going.

- **You are HEALING.** Every day you are one step closer to a healthier life. It might not feel like it during your treatments, but you *are* healing, and things *will* get better.

- **You have a STORY.** Whether you choose to share that story publicly or privately, I want you to know that your voice matters.

- **You are an EDUCATOR.** You're learning the truth about your body, and you're helping to educate those around you with this new knowledge.

- **You are an INSPIRATION.** You've been through hell and back, and if you don't feel this way about yourself, let me tell you *I* am inspired by your journey.

- **You are KIND, SMART, FUNNY, CARING,** and so much more!

Everyone is unique, and maybe you won't associate with these adjectives, but I'm sure you get the point. What makes you, *you*? I promise you, it's not Lyme disease. It's also not your career, how much money you make, or whether you're single, married, or a parent. You are *you* for the reasons that people want to be your friend. You are *you* for the reasons that people love you. I might not know you personally, but I can assure you that you are so much more than Lyme disease.

Healing is Not Linear

I've said repeatedly, there's usually a lot of trial and error as you seek treatment for Lyme disease. I hope I've also made it clear that healing from Lyme is a marathon, not a sprint, and marathons take time. As covered in the treatments chapter, the time frame for healing is different for everyone, but I want you to know that whatever your journey looks like, you need to keep fighting, no matter the obstacles in your way. This includes relapsing.

Relapsing, I'm here to say, is *part of* healing. It sucks to hear, but it's true. You're going to get better, then worse, then better again, and during that time you might fall back into your old life patterns (to the detriment of your healing), or find that your symptoms put you just about back where you feel you started. Note that I say where you *feel* you started because if you've started any kind of treatment, you will never be back where you *actually* started. However, whether you've allowed the relapse—or it happened naturally—it's all part of the healing journey.

77

And, sometimes, your body just needs a break. In those times, it is okay to stop a treatment! Of course, consult with your doctor, but don't let anyone fool you into thinking you can't take a break to rest or regroup, or to simply have a moment to *live*. There have been times in my journey where everything was just too much. Even if the treatments were working, which I know they were, I couldn't deal with the die-off symptoms, and I wasn't at a point in my life where I could commit 100% to healing. I lived alone, I was taking care of a puppy, and occasionally I still had to go into work. So, as I mentioned earlier on, at one point I stopped treatments for a while, and picked back up a few months later. This is your life, your journey, and you get to decide how it's going to look.

The Lyme Community

The Lyme community has been a lifesaver for me, but it's also important to note that support groups aren't all the same, and you might have to try a few before you find your fit. But surrounding yourself with people who "get it" is *so* important. They won't question your symptoms, and if anything, they'll validate everything you've been feeling. The friends I've made in the online Lyme community have become family. It was the greatest feeling, finally connecting with others who were experiencing the same things. They mirrored back that these symptoms were real, that I wasn't crazy, and I wasn't alone. As it turned out, my symptoms were actually quite common—no matter what my doctors made me feel for so many of years. Lyme caused things as tiny and random as puffy gums, and as severe as GI imbalances and mental health issues. The Lyme community gets it when no one else does, so I highly suggest checking out the many such support groups online.

But as I said, not every group is right for everyone, just like you won't be friends with every person you meet in life. It's important to find a group you connect with. But be wary of people who are "one upping" each other, because this isn't a competition about being the most sick. That attitude is destructive, and will keep you in the mentality of being sick, rather than working to heal. Also, many people will give unwarranted advice about how they healed. Oftentimes, those people are so excited to share what worked for them that they're shouting it from the rooftop! It's my belief that they really do want to help others, but sometimes people have the mindset that it's "their way or the highway." At this point you know everyone's journey is different, so remember that when certain types of people put "other" treatments down, those exact treatments might be just the ones that'll heal you best.

It's also okay to leave a group at any time, for any reason. Setting personal boundaries is really important! It's a lesson I've had to learn the hard way. Many people with Lyme have the personality trait of being a "people pleaser," and so tend to put more energy into what *others* think than into figuring out how *they* feel. I'm this way, and so I have to work hard to set boundaries with myself, including how much energy I contribute to a Lyme group. Also, some groups, frankly, have a lot of "Debbie Downers." When group members aren't cheering for your success but seem to be cheering for you to keep feeling ill, you're in the wrong group! We so easily fall into the trap of being a victim, and even get praise for it. Our society is backwards in this way—particularly as it pertains to women. Think about the "Damsel In Distress": it's a woman, distraught or in danger, who can't fend for herself and needs a man to save her. This image has bombarded most of us from a very young age. Nearly every fairytale has this type of narrative, so it makes sense that people might perceive themselves this way. What I'm trying to get at is that we need to be the valiant hero of our own stories, and once we're in control of that narrative, we can then help others. There are many groups filled with positive and encouraging Lyme warriors, so keep searching for one until you feel it's right for you. Your healing journey depends on it, and your body will thank you later.

Break the Monotony of Your Day

It's so easy to get into a "rut" when you battle Lyme disease. Too often, we find ourselves doing the same thing, day in and day out, usually because we're scared of change. Having a routine can be great, especially when it comes to taking your medications, but if you find yourself "stuck in a loop," where every day looks the same, I encourage you to try and change it up. Many people who experienced the COVID-19 lockdowns can relate to this too, because we were all stuck at home with basically nothing to do but entertain ourselves. And that got pretty boring, pretty quickly. It's not even about whether life is boring or not, it's the effect that our monotonous schedules have on our minds. When you have nothing to look forward to throughout your week, it's much easier to sink into a depression than it is to find joy.

Now I also want to mention that sometimes we *need* order and a strict schedule—perhaps especially when first starting a new Lyme treatment protocol. The number of medications and supplements we end up taking can be overwhelming and honestly, it can take up the entire day just trying to take them before food, with food, and hours away from food. So, taking time to fit your new protocol into your daily life is important, but it's what you do in between medications that can help you change up the monotony. Let's say you're working a full-time job, and your only free time is in the evening, but every evening finds you exhausted from work, and all you want to do is curl up and watch mindless TV. That's perfectly valid! That can be a form a self-care, and I can honestly say I spend many nights like this. But it doesn't mean it has to be every night, and I'd hope not every weekend when you find yourself having more time. When you have that free time, I want to encourage you to actively make a change in your schedule; to add in something you enjoy doing, but haven't done in a while, and see how your mood changes.

Changing up your routine does not have to mean physical changes; it can also be mindfulness tweaks, and other things you can do from the comfort of your home. Here are some activities, both physical and not, that you can try adding to your week to break up the monotony:

- Get outside and go for a walk.

- Join a support group that meets once a week, online or in person.

- Join a book club, or choose to read a new book every month.

- Grab coffee at a coffee shop one morning, instead of brewing it yourself.

- Try arts and crafts like a paint by numbers, a puzzle, coloring in a coloring book, etc.

• Join a yoga class or a fitness program you enjoy, whether in person or online. If you have physical limitations, a stretching class or breathwork class can also be really beneficial.

• Go out to dinner once a week or have a dinner party with friends, at your place or theirs.

• Do a DIY spa-night every week, where you do a face mask, a mani/pedi, or whatever else makes you feel relaxed and peaceful.

• Have a game night with your friends every week or so, either in person or online.

• Go to the movies, or have a movie night with friends at home.

• Travel to a new place, whether it's a beach, park, or garden. Take in the new sights and see how beautiful our world is. If you can't drive, have a friend drive you, check out public transportation, or mark it on your schedule for a future date that you can look forward to.

It really doesn't matter what you do to change up your monotonous schedule, just as long as you are incorporating things you love and can look forward to, every week. Sometimes simply getting out of the house—or even putting on regular clothes, some makeup, or styling your hair, can make a difference. Personally, it can change my mood nearly instantly, helping me feel better. Even when I'm flaring, sometimes I feel immensely improved when I make the effort to change up my day. If you can't change your schedule right now, for whatever reason, try to plan for something in the future so you can visualize what a great day it'll be. Should you have to cancel the plan last minute, so be it—at least you took an actionable step in trying to make that happen! It's important to change up the monotony as best you can because, at least for me, it's really helped put things into perspective. It's allowed me to establish a positive and grateful mindset because I'm able to get outside myself and my own story, and see how much the world has to offer. Battling Lyme can be lonely, but you don't need to live your life alone!

Having a Positive Mindset vs. Toxic Positivity

Having the right mindset is extremely important when it comes to healing from a chronic illness, but there's a difference between staying positive and having toxic positivity. You, and you alone, are the only person who can determine your outlook on life. It's a choice you'll have to make, and it's not always easy. Staying positive throughout this journey can be difficult, because everything seems to be against us. But having a positive mindset does not mean you have to be positive every hour of every day. There are days when crying it out is exactly what you need to do. Many people think staying positive means avoiding their pain, as well as any other feelings that might arise. This is not what you should be doing, as it's a sign that someone's positivity has become toxic. Our bodies hold onto trauma, and the more you resist how you truly feel, the more you'll suppress those emotions. They'll get trapped inside your body, and it'll become harder and harder to clear them out. So, avoiding pain and faking a smile is never the answer. The key to having a positive mindset is much larger than that. It has to do with the overall picture of how you view your life. Having a positive mindset can be hard, so here are some things you can do, every day, to help you achieve one:

1. Have a gratitude journal or notepad on your phone, and write down a few things that you're grateful for every day. The more you do this, the more your brain will start to look out for things to be grateful for. Is there something you're able to do today that you weren't able to do yesterday, or last week, or last month? Maybe you were able to eat food today and not feel sick. Maybe you were able to take a walk around your neighborhood, or maybe you sat outside and listened to the birds chirping and realized how beautiful nature is. There's nothing too small to be grateful for. Many days I'm just grateful that I've survived it, and that's something to be grateful for, no matter what.

2. Focus more on what you're able to do, than on your limitations. What you think about, talk about, and even read can determine your mindset. The more your brain focuses on something, the more it gives that particular thing power.

3. Your yesterday does not determine your today or tomorrow. Know that healing is not linear, and nothing lasts forever. Life changes for us all, for better and worse, and realizing that healing from Lyme is not a race will help keep things in perspective.

Another step toward healthy positivity is *learning*: learning to live in a healthy and happy state. And this means we need to actively retrain our brains to help us toward this goal. As I mentioned earlier, Lyme disease affects the brain in many ways, including causing conditions like anxiety, depression, depersonalization, and much more. Talk about a game-changer. Realizing that many of my negative thoughts weren't my fault was incredibly helpful. It allowed me to internalize that I had a chemical imbalance from the Lyme spirochetes flaring up or dying. I found myself spiraling into negative thoughts all the time, and it wasn't until I realized *it was the bugs and not me* that I could actively work to change them. And that's when I started seeing results and getting better. Retraining the limbic system can be hard work, but following a "brain rewiring" program, as I mentioned in the "Treatments" section, can really help! I've been following The Gupta Program, and have found the daily meditations and seven-step approach (a physical stepping pattern they teach you) to really help alleviate my anxiety, lesson any symptoms I might be experiencing, and help me remember that negative thoughts are "just a loop in the brain," as Ashok Gupta calls it. It's worth repeating that the brain can easily get stuck in a chronically ill state, so retraining it to focus on health and happiness can be crucial for one's healing. I've also known people to heal from Lyme disease, mold toxicity, mast cell activation syndrome (MCAS) and more, simply by following a brain rewiring program! That's how powerful our brains are!

Now that we've talked about having a healthy mindset, I want to talk a bit more about toxic positivity. As I touched on earlier, it's not healthy or normal to feel happy 100% of the time. We're human, and we're designed to feel everything. There are days when we're sad, mad, hurt, frustrated, and discouraged. Do not avoid these feelings in order to try and stay positive. People who tell you otherwise will eventually hit a wall and have a much harder time bouncing back from it. And everything you see on social media is simply a curated glimpse into someone else's life. It's a highlight reel, not the entire story. I try to show both my good days and my bad days on my accounts, but naturally I want to focus on happy moments and share pretty pictures of myself. This is normal and, like I said before, it's good to focus on the positives. But I'm also not avoiding the painful days, and I'm certainly not pretending that they don't exist. It's easy to compare yourself to others on social media; to feel like you have to put on an act in order to fit in. This can be toxic. The best thing you can ever do is to be your authentic self. So choose positivity over negativity, and be grateful for what you *do* have.

You've probably heard the phrase, "fake it till you make it." Now, I do agree this can be useful at times, and it helps us to feel confident, but when it comes to healing, I think it straddles a fine line between helping and hurting us. This is also when I see toxic positivity arise. When we "fake" feeling happy and healthy, it usually means we're suppressing how we truly feel, and when we do that, we bury those real and painful emotions deep inside us. The more we "fake it," the deeper down our true feelings hide. When it comes to healing, we want to feel happy and healthy for real—not just pretend to be in that state of mind. Now, I do agree that consciously choosing to smile and laugh can be a good thing because it naturally boosts serotonin and dopamine levels in our brain. One exception: when someone else is telling you to "smile more." In that case you can kindly tell them to F off! Only you get to choose how you feel each day. So I think it's less about "faking it till you make it," and more about the consistent practice of choosing to feel happy, healthy, confident, worthy, loved, etc. The more you can feel those emotions, the more your body will naturally default to that setting.

Setting Boundaries

Setting boundaries can be hard for many people. I have a hard time with it for sure, but it's a form of self-care that isn't talked about enough. You simply cannot be there for someone else when you yourself are completely drained. Setting boundaries is an important part of your healing journey, and this will include setting them with family, friends, partners, and coworkers. It's not a selfish act, but it might feel that way because many people are programmed to be "yes" people. But saying "no" shouldn't be viewed as a bad thing.

As I've said, I have a hard time saying "no," especially when it comes to helping others. In the past, I've completely drained my energy trying to help people, like on social media, by trying to answer every single message in a timely manner, no matter how I was feeling or where my energy was at. It would make me flare. But knowing I was helping others, that I was "being there" for them, was what made me keep pushing myself. Here's the thing, though: If you aren't focusing on your own well-being, you're not going to be of much help to anyone else. So, despite my best efforts, I would eventually hit a wall and no longer be able to respond to anyone at all. Today, rather than wear myself thin, I know it's okay to take a break and tell others I'll get back to them when I can. For the most part, the only person putting pressure on me to answer messages immediately was me.

The same logic goes for in-person interactions as well. I found myself saying "yes" to every birthday party, improv show, and happy hour because I wanted to be a good friend. But if someone told me they weren't feeling well and they were using all their strength to make an appearance at my party, I'd be upset! I'd never want someone jeopardizing his/her/their own health for me, and I have to constantly remind myself of this for my own well-being. The bottom line is, it's okay to say, "no"! Your health needs to be your #1 priority, and don't let anyone tell you otherwise.

Saying "no" can feel icky. I get it. So, let's work on ways to do so without feeling like a bad person, or a bad friend. That's why I suggest you think of a "no" as a "not now." Every relationship is different, and you'll know best how to communicate with your own friends, family, and colleagues but, in general, I've found it helpful to be honest and upfront. If you've really not been feeling well, or feel like every day is different, I'd suggest telling your friend something like "things might change based on how I'm feeling" when confirming your attendance at their event. Giving people a heads up that you might have to bail will feel better than cancelling last minute. Sometimes this isn't possible because a flare might come on right when you've been feeling great for weeks, or even months. So, if that's the case, don't beat yourself up for saying no! If you have to bail last minute, simply do it; don't stress over it, and move on. However, just because we have an illness doesn't give us permission to not communicate. So be sure you *tell* your friend that you're not coming. A true friend will understand, and if they don't, they probably aren't as good a friend as you thought.

Also, there's something I like to call a "partial yes." It's like saying, "Yes, I'd like to attend your activity, but there are some boundaries I'll need to establish in order to attend." These could be related to a time limit—like, maybe you'll only commit to one hour at the party, so you'll drive there either on your own or with someone who knows that you'll be leaving early. Creating a personal boundary that works for you might allow you to attend something you'd otherwise have to pass on. When battling Lyme, it's important that we make adjustments to our schedules when needed, but it doesn't mean everything is a hard "yes" or "no." You can also have a "partial no," as when you'd love to go, but it's not possible unless the activity changes in some way. Or, as I mentioned earlier, it can be a "not now," which is also a "partial no."

Now, I'll admit that I've seen a lot of friends "ghost" each other, meaning not respond to any texts or calls, rather than speaking their truth. Sometimes we can't fully communicate what we're feeling, which is understandable. But I think everyone needs to give the people in their life more credit. The bottom line is, you are an amazing human being, and you deserve to give and receive proper communication. Don't always take the "easier" way out and not respond (or not show up). Even healthy people have a hard time saying "no," so I encourage you to tap into the warrior that you are, put on your big person pants, and communicate how you're feeling as best you can. In the end, the right people will stick around.

Boundaries can also change throughout your healing journey. Just because you can't have a night out right now, doesn't mean you won't be able to in a few months. As I said before, healing is not linear, and you will have great days and bad days. Days when you can hang out with friends, and days when you need to stay home alone, watching Netflix. Setting boundaries is personal, and different for everyone. What works for me won't necessarily work for you. I'm an extravert, and sometimes I feel better when I get out of the house and meet up with friends for a walk. Sometimes the change of scenery and distraction from whatever

I'm feeling is just what I needed. Other times, I need to isolate myself, detox from social media, and just be with my emotions. There are days when I have to put myself first, and don't call a friend back right away because their venting might push me over the edge. And that's nothing I ever did in the past. I was always the friend who was available to talk, listen, and rant to. But the longer I've been on this journey, the more I've realized how much energy gets sucked out of me on calls like this. That's a personal boundary I set for myself from time to time. And you know what? Those friends haven't abandoned me. If I tell them I'll call them back, I *will* call them back. So I encourage you to think about your own boundaries, and make sure you're putting your health and healing first.

Dealing with Those Who Don't Get It

You might have heard the phrase, "people don't get it, until they get it." This is true for many things in life, especially Lyme disease. You'll never know how someone feels until you walk in his, her, or their shoes, and honestly it's not always possible. So how do we deal with people who won't ever "get it"? I have a few tips to share—ones that have helped me. After battling an invisible illness for 12 years, I've realized that at the end of the day, most people truly want to help, but many don't know how. Now, there are others who will consistently deny that Lyme or chronic Lyme exists, and those people, in my opinion, are uneducated and in denial. So, whether you're dealing with someone who is struggling to understand what you're going through, or someone who's dismissing your experience all together, here are a few ways to cope and, ideally, keep your sanity during such interactions.

First, it helps to remind yourself that they don't know how you feel. It might be hard to do, but I give them grace for whatever they might be saying or any "advice" they're giving. If you can get past feeling annoyed and frustrated by their comments, you might see that it's usually coming from a place of good intent. It's not always! But more often than not, I've found that most people are trying to make sense of the condition as best they can.

Second, it helps to express how *I'm feeling* and how, whatever they've just said makes *me* feel. Keeping the focus on yourself will help you avoid a confrontation. Saying things like "you don't get it," or "you have no idea how I'm feeling," doesn't help because the truth is that the person doesn't, but they also don't realize that they don't. Explaining it to them can also be exhausting. So, unless you find they're really willing to listen, *and* you have the energy to talk for a long time, I'd simply say something like "I know it might not look like it, but I'm feeling really sick today" or "thank you for your advice, but I'm sticking with the current treatment recommended by my doctor." Basically, find a polite way to move the conversation along, especially if it's not going in a direction that's beneficial for you.

Third, if the person is an internet troll (an online stranger who makes mean remarks), either don't engage, or find the humor in their comment and brush it off with a witty comment back. These people are not worth your time! I can't count the number of trolls who've told me "Lyme disease isn't real." At first, I wanted to fight them all, and to make them understand just how wrong they were. I wanted to say things like "Wait till you get bit by a tick!," or "I dare you to go walking barefoot through the forest!" Their comments made me furious, as they'd probably make you too, but why should I give them any power by interacting with them? That's what they want. They want the fight. And we fight enough every day. We fight for our health! So don't let uneducated opinions get to you. You know your body, you know Lyme is real, and if you ever doubt it, I'm here to remind you that your feelings are valid, your illness is real, and I believe you. Ignore the haters, because as Taylor Swift says, "Haters gonna hate."

How to Help People Understand

This chapter is meant for close friends and family. You'll never be able to make everyone understand what you're going through. Most people won't "get it"—and it's not usually worth your energy or time to educate them. But there are some people in our lives who are worth trying to have difficult conversations with. These people will accept that while they might not truly understand, they are still willing to support you as best they can. These are the people who want to learn and understand what it is you're going through, and will help amplify your voice. They're the listeners; the ones who don't question everything you talk about. They will have the wherewithal to understand, at least to some degree, what it is that Lyme warriors go through. So, here's how you can help them on their learning journey, on the days when you have the energy to do so.

Start with the kernel they *do* understand. Do they understand the physical pain? Maybe they have arthritis, or a sports injury from the past. Maybe they've had a bad case of the flu? While it's not identical to what a Lyme warrior goes through, it can be a starting point for someone to relate to what you're saying. For instance, let's say they had tendonitis as a teenager. You can say something like, "Remember when you had tendonitis, and were in a lot of pain sophomore year? That's similar to how I feel almost every day. It might not always look like I'm in pain, but that's because I've built up a really high pain tolerance and am simply trying to live my life." I've found that if someone can physically relate to a time in their life where they had similar symptoms, then that person will have more empathy and understanding for what you're going through. So analogies can be helpful. However they don't always work, especially if the person has had no real trauma in his/her/their life. Lucky them. So what next?

You can paint a picture for them visually. Even if they've never experienced what you're about to describe, they'll certainly be able to comprehend it. For instance, if your pain is a 10 out of 10, and you're really fatigued, you might say something like, "Today I feel like I ran a marathon. You can't see it, but every single one of my joints and muscles hurts." Even if that person has not run a marathon, they should know how difficult and taxing it is on the human body. Another option might be: "I feel like I got hit by a truck." I sure hope they haven't been hit by a truck, but everyone's seen a truck, and should be able to imagine the pain it would cause if it hit them. Unfortunately, there will still be people that won't grasp what you're saying because your symptoms are "invisible." Those people are hard to get through to, but it's not impossible.

Consider other things that people can't see, but know exist. Maybe they believe in God. Or maybe they invest money in stocks and bonds.

In both cases, someone knows something is "there," but they cannot physically see it. Remember: People will have trouble understanding someone else's pain if they can't find a way to relate to it.

Another approach is to help educate someone by sending them information about Lyme disease. If they like reading, there are tons of books about Lyme, and what a patient goes through (you're reading one right now!). There are also great documentaries that show how debilitating symptoms can be, and how every person battling Lyme has a different story. I really like showing people the documentary *Under Our Skin*. It does a great job of illustrating the views of patients, doctors, and caregivers. And it's helpful when your friend or family member has more than one story of Lyme to look at, as the more information people have about something, the more they tend to believe it.

Last but not least, please know it is not your job to make someone understand. You can't change them, their thoughts, or their beliefs. They have to be open and willing to put the effort in themselves. My suggestions are ways you may be able to guide people on their journey toward understanding. But all we can do is communicate, openly and honestly, and then it's on them. The goal is for our loved ones to have compassion and empathy for what we go through. For them to get a glimpse into the pain and struggle we deal with every day. And for them to believe us. They'll never fully understand. But whether they "get it" or not, they can believe, support, and love you, just as you are. It's not your job to "fix" the situation. You have to let go of how you want them to feel, and just be okay with however they do. Focus on yourself, keep the loved ones who believe you close, and everyone else at a bit of a distance.

How to Love a Body That Doesn't Love You Back

Loving a body that doesn't work the way it's "supposed" to; that feels like it's "failed" you in every way possible, is hard to do. And it's okay if you don't. I've been there, I'm still there, and I get it. I also want to note from the start that ableism is a huge issue in our world, and I'm going to try my best to write an inclusive chapter surrounding this topic. Ability does not determine whether a person is deserving of love and acceptance! Many days, I still struggle with loving myself, but I've come to realize and accept that my body is beautiful just the way it is. I also recognize that some bodies do indeed need to be "fixed," and that some people are actively looking for effective treatments to do just that. I work hard at having body positivity, but body neutrality is just as valid! The bottom line is that your health does not determine your worth—nor does your attitude about your body!

We only get one body and one life, and no matter what battle you're facing, your body is worthy of love and acceptance. Bodies are bodies. Every shape, form, and color. Bodies are meant to sustain us, but some people's bodies actively harm them. And when that's the case, it can lead to complicated feelings. And even those not in love with their bodies deserve to heal. As I hold space for those who feel this way, here's how I've learned to love and accept my own body, even when it doesn't always love me back.

My body is a fighter, and with that comes battle scars and physical and emotional wounds of all kinds. Post-Traumatic Stress Disorder (PTSD) also comes with wounds, wounds from the trauma of being dismissed by doctors and family members for more than a decade. But this is me, and this is my body. I used to get so angry about being sick, because everything felt out of my control. And many days my symptoms are *still* out of my control. But what I *can* control is the way in which I deal with them. Being chronically ill for years has shown me that symptoms are not the same every day, and sometimes not even every hour. So, each day I try to find something in my body to be grateful for. My body works so hard for me, and even though I might be in pain, my body wants to heal. And even when I'm not actively thinking about healing, my body is working to heal itself.

Changing the narrative that runs through our minds each day is extremely important. Do you find yourself saying things like, "my body is broken," or "my body hates me," or "I can't do that because I'm too sick"? Your feelings are valid, but negative thinking will trap you in a vicious cycle that is hard to break. Ever hear someone say, "what you think and say becomes your reality"? Well, even if it sounds far-fetched, it's true. If you're putting all your mental and physical energy into saying you're sick, that's what you're going to think about, and subconsciously feel, all the time. So, first and foremost, you need to change the way you talk to yourself. Every day you need to send love to your body; and if not love, acceptance. Especially on the days when you're flaring and don't want to. I'm not saying it's easy to do, but it's important to send love and healing energy to those parts of your body that are in pain. Yes, I'm asking you to send love to Lyme disease, and parasites too! Send loving thoughts while asking those critters to kindly get the F out! Love is at our core, it's our human nature. Even when our bodies are chronically ill, they are desperately seeking love, just like every other being.

In the same way, we must surrender to whatever our bodies are doing at that present moment. We need to surrender to our healing, knowing it won't happen exactly the way we think it will, and surrender to every feeling and symptom that arises in us. Being chronically ill does not make you any less worthy than a "healthy" person. We are all made "perfectly imperfect," and it's our flaws that make us unique. Now, you might be thinking, "I don't want to be unique, I want to be normal!" and I get that. Embracing the parts of ourselves that we think are "ugly" or "sick" is really hard to do. But I can assure you that even the most beautiful person on this planet has had body issues and insecurities, at one point or another. No one is perfect! Perfect doesn't exist. Even when people try to define perfect, everyone has a different answer. What one person finds "perfect" is someone else's "ugly."

So, picture this for a moment: Think about all your "flaws" and the things you dislike about your body. Those flaws are what make you a fighter. The body's ability to "do" something does not define its worth. It's hard not to wish for a healthy body when our world is designed for one, but being grateful for what we do have, assisted or unassisted, can make all the difference. Life is short, and bodies are odd—beautifully, unfathomably, and wonderfully odd. We only get the one, so let's make the most of it and try to love and accept ourselves exactly as we are.

Learning to Rest

As I said in an earlier chapter, resting is not doing "nothing"! There's a huge misconception around this that I'm eager to address further. Whether you're battling Lyme yourself, or whether you're an ally, the pressure put on a chronically ill person to "just do it" or to "just get up and get moving" can be extremely harmful. Resting is what allows our bodies to heal! If you're experiencing extreme fatigue, your body is trying to tell you something. I can't stress this enough. It's important to start noticing what your body is telling you, and to stop fearing that you're "missing out" on life. It's hard! I get it, trust me, I still feel this way—a lot. You may have heard of the "Spoon Theory," and if not, here is a brief recap. Christine Miserandino, an award-winning writer and chronic illness warrior, battling Lupus, came up with this wonderful metaphor for people dealing with chronic illnesses, and their limitations; and a way to be mindful of the energy you expend, to better make it through each day. In her personal story titled "The Spoon Theory" (which you can read on her website butyoudontlooksick.com), she writes that everyone has a certain number of "spoons" (spoons represent energy) they have access to every day. For example, she also does a great job of explaining how a simple shower can take up a certain amount of spoons for someone with a chronic illness, whereas a healthier person might find that none of their spoons have been depleted. I love this metaphor but, personally, I don't calculate my "spoons" every day. Though it can be really helpful for some! And it can help explain to loved ones why some days you feel endless energy and some days, none at all. I have an okay time with my energy levels, and have found that instead of helping, tracking my "spoons" puts me in a fearful mindset, imagining that a simple activity might completely deplete me. This isn't always the case, but I decided to stop tracking them. Still, I do recommend taking a look at her method! This is why we call each other "spoonies," and if you have Lyme, you are certainly part of our Spoonie-hood.

So though I don't track my "spoons," I still make the time to rest when I need to. And if there's a day where I'm like, "why am I extra tired or fatigued?" I'll think back to yesterday and remember, "oh, I did X, Y, and Z, and that's probably too much on my body and so, I need to rest." As I mentioned earlier, I've always been a "go, go, go" person. People will often describe me as the Energizer Bunny. So resting is not something that came naturally to me—I've had to work at it! What's helped me the most is to realize that resting is not a passive activity. Choosing to rest is an active choice, which gets me back to my original point. Resting is not doing "nothing," it's doing one of the most important "somethings" you can do to heal.

So, please understand that you are not being lazy if you choose to rest. Far from it. In order to get out of that mindset, or to explain to others why you're resting, here are a few ways you can switch around the narrative. Think about it like this:

• You are replenishing your energy levels, so you can be present later on.

• Your body is fighting hard for you, so you're giving it the time and space it needs.

• You are putting your health first.

• Resting today does not mean you'll need to rest tomorrow.

Comparison Kills

Comparing ourselves to others, both to healthier friends and chronically ill friends, is never the thing to do. For better or worse, your healing journey will naturally have its ups and downs—and it *will* get better. I want to dive a little deeper into why it's important not to compare ourselves to others, and I'll start first with our more able-bodied friends.

It's normal to grieve our past selves; to remember what it was like before you had a chronic illness. It's hard adjusting to your new normal, whether it's temporary or permanent, but just because someone might seem healthier than you, doesn't mean they have a better life. It's similar to admiring celebrities and imagining that they have perfect lives—just because someone has unlimited material possessions and wealth, doesn't secure them happiness. Now, you're probably thinking, "I would give anything not to deal with this illness," and I don't blame you. I actually wish that for you as well! But the fact is, we're handed certain cards in life, many of which are out of our control, and it's how we deal with those cards that matters. This goes for every single human, ill or not, because it's not about what life gives you, but what you do with what you're given.

We also don't want to compare ourselves to other Lyme warriors. This is really important because once we start doing that, we stray from our own path, and might even go against what our doctors are advising us to do because "so-and-so friend" is doing something else, and having better success. It's great and important to take note of the treatments that work for your peers, but comparing yourself to them doesn't accomplish anything or reveal any "truth." You have no idea where they are in their journey (even if you do, you probably don't *fully* know), and the specific treatment they're doing might only have worked after years spent doing something else. I'll repeat: Every treatment you go through is part of your path to remission, and part of the bigger plan. It might aid you in pivoting to a different protocol, or help with one of your various symptoms—and that's still something. That means everything you do is worth it and part of your path to remission.

Remember too that Lyme disease is different for every single person. Some people's main symptoms might be migraines, so their journey can't be comparable to mine, which has been filled mostly with gastrointestinal issues and nausea. We're different people, with different manifestations of Lyme, who require different treatments to heal! I so wish that Lyme was a straightforward illness that could be treated the same way for each person out there, in order to reach remission, but that's not how it is. We're unique and beautiful warriors, each with a voice that matters and a story to tell. So don't measure your success based on someone else. If getting out of bed is your "win" for the day, celebrate that! If eating food and not getting sick is your "win," celebrate that, too! Don't let anyone else dull your joy because they "seem" to be doing so much better. As you know, our symptoms are often invisible, so you can never truly know what someone else is going through. Stick to your path, let your friends stick to theirs, and root for each other along the way!

Dating with Lyme

If you're single, you'll know that dating today has its own challenges. Then throw in a chronic illness and it can feel overwhelming. I know this feeling all too well. But, at the end of the day, everyone has their own struggles. So you're battling Lyme disease, okay, cool! Allow me to repeat: You are not your diagnosis. Just because someone is healthy, does not mean they don't have "baggage" of their own. Yes, dealing with a chronic illness can be a lot, especially during treatments, but once you realize how awesome you are, and how deserving and worthy you are of love, you can delve into how to communicate about Lyme when you go on dates.

To start, opening up about Lyme disease is personal, and you should only share that information when you feel comfortable. I tend to share about it early on, within the first few dates or messages, because it's been such an important part of my life. But not everyone is an open book, and that's okay. I've also had bad experiences opening up about Lyme disease when first meeting someone. Some guys have completely ghosted me, or unmatched with me on dating sites. What I say is: Those guys are shitty and not worth my time! Did I cry and eat junk food? Maybe—but really, their actions have helped me weed out who's a keeper and who isn't. I've also had really great experiences when I've mentioned Lyme early on. I've found it can work to break the ice and get us past small talk, which is always nice. No matter when you decide to mention Lyme, I encourage you not to be ashamed of it.

That said, I also encourage you to phrase your Lyme diagnosis in a positive light. Rather than saying "I have Lyme disease," try saying "I am healing from Lyme disease," or "I'm currently battling Lyme disease." Life isn't black and white, and Lyme certainly isn't either. There's really no need to dwell on the negative aspects of Lyme when mentioning it to someone new. And remember, everyone has something they're not comfortable sharing right away. Or something they feel bad about. At the end of the day, the right people will come along, and the wrong people will move on. That's life. Illness or not. All we can do is be the best version of ourselves, and know that the right person is going to love us for who we are.

So, to recap, **1) Share about your Lyme journey when it feels best to you, and don't be ashamed of your story. 2) Focus on the fact that you're healing. And 3) Know that the right person is out there.** Anyone who doesn't work out is just helping you clear the path for the person who will stick around for good.

Another big part of dating with Lyme disease is the physical limitations. Many people feel restricted when they battle Lyme, and I think it can be confusing how to proceed, even if you're able to date. Still, anything is possible. That said, it's okay if you aren't up for dating. If you are, however, I have some suggestions. I am forever grateful for technology, which is my first tip. Virtual dates are a thing and can be GREAT! I'm writing this book during COVID-19 times, and yet I've been on a bunch of (virtual) dates. Video calls are a great way to get to know someone when you are physically unable to leave the house. This is just one example of why I think it's so important to focus on what we *can* do, not what we can't. We have to be open to all kinds of possibilities, opportunities, and different kinds of dates. Even if you aren't bedbound, someone battling Lyme often deals with a lot of physical limitations, and I don't want this to hold you back from dating. It just means that dating might look different for you than for your friends. More virtual dates, video calls, and nights in, rather than nights out. Or if you do go out, maybe it's for a picnic in a park, where there's little walking and you can bring your own food. Dating can and does work when you have Lyme! Sometimes you just have to get creative with your dates, and make sure you're listening to your body and not pushing yourself too hard.

Now, let's talk about being intimate with your partner. There are not enough studies on this, but some people believe that Lyme can be sexually transmitted and even passed on, in utero, to an unborn child. I know people who have experienced both, and we know how accurate the CDC's info is (for those that don't remember, they don't think chronic Lyme exists). So, as a word of advice, in order to protect others, use protection. It's that simple. Also, most of the Lyme community agrees that Lyme is only transmittable when it's an active infection. If it's dormant, this doesn't seem to be an issue! Does this bring up another potentially awkward conversation when dating? Yup. But the principles that apply are similar to the ones I mentioned before. **1) Bring this up when you feel comfortable. 2) Everyone has "baggage," and things they're nervous to talk about. 3) The right person isn't going to care, and will respect your wishes to be safe. And 4), when Lyme is dormant, this doesn't seem to be an issue.** Pregnancy is another topic, but many Lyme doctors can help discuss options for moving forward with a healthy pregnancy! A good friend of mine is currently in remission from Lyme and has a healthy pregnancy, and is thriving.

This is all to say that yes, you can have an amazing dating life while battling chronic Lyme disease, and yes you can have a future and the family you've always dreamed of. Everyone is different, so of course continue to consult with your doctor on all matters, but also don't let the fear of the unknown run your life. You are worthy of your deepest desires, and I encourage you to embrace change, stay positive, and keep fighting for everything you believe in. Don't let Lyme hold you back. And to the people who don't see that in you, let them go. One final note: Let go of any timeline when it comes to dating. Your journey is unique to you, and you're exactly where you're supposed to be at this given moment.

Being in a Relationship with Lyme

Okay, so you know you're worthy of love, and you've found someone who agrees, yay! That's huge, and such an exciting journey to be on. Having been in a serious relationship myself while being chronically ill, I know there are issues that can arise, and that most of them revolve around communication. So, once you've gotten past the point of explaining to him/her/them that you have Lyme disease, don't be surprised if you start having some unpleasant feelings. For example, feeling like a burden, wondering how to separate yourself from your diagnosis, not knowing how to get your partner to better understand what you're going through, learning how to have patience when they don't, how to find the sexy, and dealing with past trauma around relationships that didn't work out. These are all valid issues, and even common when in a relationship. I'm going to give you some advice on all of them, but it's really important to note that even people who aren't chronically ill go through similar stages because being in a relationship can be hard even if you don't have Lyme disease. Yes, Lyme can make things more difficult, but I'm really trying to encourage you to stop viewing yourself as a victim. Those feelings are so, so valid, but you are also so much more than any negative thought running through your head!

First, let's talk about feeling like a burden. Do you have some limitations in your life right now? Probably. But do they make you any less deserving of love? No. I've found that we often put great pressure on ourselves to be healthy, and that when we aren't, we automatically view this as a negative impact on a relationship. But, news flash, this chapter is about *already being* in a relationship, so that person (hopefully) already knows you have Lyme, and it's not stopping them from wanting to be with you. Of course, knowing that isn't likely to stop you from feeling like a burden from time to time. Honestly, I still feel this way whether I'm in a relationship or not. Living with Lyme is hard, and it's normal to want more for your life and for your relationship. But I've found that the sensation of being a "burden" usually comes directly from the patient, and not from their partner. It's part of the victim mentality we may develop, and it's a type of self-sabotage. Typically, we don't mean to do this but, being chronically ill, it's easy to fall into a cycle of bad habits such as these. So, how do you resist? It starts with being vulnerable and communicating the feeling you're having to your partner. Relationships aren't transactional, and even if there are things you can't do that your partner can, you still bring value to the relationship. Therapy can definitely help as well. Again: I'm not a therapist, but working on your own self-worth—and then communicating openly with your partner about these feelings—will help you to debunk them. I can sit here and write a million times "you're not a burden, you're not a burden, you're not a burden," but it won't matter until you start to believe it yourself. So, know that your partner wants to be with you despite the fact that you have Lyme, that he/she/they *want* to help you, and that any limitations you have right now are just part of your path.

Now let's talk about separating yourself from your diagnosis. We cling to labels to feel safe and heard, and this goes for everyone in life.

If you were to ask someone, *who are you?*, I bet their first response would be to tell you what they do for work. Then maybe they'd mention their religion, and whether they're married and have kids. So, does your job, religion, and family define who you are as a person? No, because what happens when all of that is stripped away? Who were you before you had that job, before your religion, and before you had a family? You were *you*. Yes, you might enjoy some of those labels, and even want them to define you, but I encourage you to let them go for a minute. So, let's take Lyme out of the equation as well. Who are you? What are your passions and hobbies? What makes you smile, and what makes you cry? Who's the person you want people to see you as? These are what make up who you are, and they're probably why your partner is in a relationship with you. Yes, Lyme can sometimes take up the whole picture, and that's okay. Sometimes we have to shift our focus, take a step back, and remember who we were before getting diagnosed to remember what truly defines us.

Still, sometimes it feels like our partner can't truly understand what we're going through. That's going to happen, and it's important to have patience as he/she/they process it all. But cultivating patience is hard, especially if you don't have the energy to constantly explain yourself. Earlier, I talked about getting people to better understand Lyme and your experience with the disease, but when it comes to a relationship, it's a lot more personal. Your partner will see you at your worst, and will experience the effects Lyme can have on you, nearly firsthand. At these times, it's important to remember how difficult it is for our caregivers to watch us go through challenging treatments and flare-ups. Sure, it's not the same as going through it as a patient, but it's still difficult, and we need to have grace for our loved ones. Again, it comes down to communication, and being vulnerable. Your partner might see your physical pain, but if you're not already aware of this, Lyme warriors have a special skill called "hiding how we're really feeling." We're great at it because it's a survival mechanism we need, just to keep living. But it's important to let down your guard and be open with your loved ones. That's the best chance you can give them to see what it is you're going through. Being vulnerable isn't easy! It takes work, but as you work this "muscle," you'll get better at embracing the discomfort that comes with the territory. Also, it's important to recognize that most fights are caused by miscommunication, and so aren't really about either of you. Open communication can sometimes reveal that you're both fighting over the desire to be healthy, and to not have to deal with a chronic illness symptom or situation. I encourage you to keep giving yourselves a break, because battling an illness is hard and being in a relationship takes work. Be patient with each other, and remember the reasons you fell in love in the first place.

So, once you feel able to be vulnerable and communicate honestly with your partner, what happens when they still don't "get it"? Well, it's easy to become impatient and snap, and say things like "you'll never understand." Because, yeah, they won't, but acting that way will ensure that they won't even want to. Lyme can cause radical mood swings, so the "you" who snaps is really just "you in that moment," not the *real you*. That's okay, it happens. Your partner also might snap from time to time. Again, living with Lyme is hard for everyone that experiences it, first or secondhand. So, how can you maintain patience? It starts with having patience with yourself. You're going to be angry at your symptoms, and frustrated when you realize you aren't better yet. I'm angry and frustrated for you! And, I can assure you, so is your partner. Knowing that everyone is on the same page when it comes to hating Lyme disease might help you connect more with your partner. So, finding ways to be vulnerable, to communicate clearly, and to accept that they can't experience Lyme firsthand, will help you find patience with your partner.

Next, I want to touch on something fun—namely, finding the sexy. There are days when you will not feel sexy. There are days when you might even hate your body, and there will certainly be days when you will hate your current situation. This is all so valid, and I hate that you're going through it. You want to know who else hates it? Your partner. But he/she/they love you for who you are, flaws and all. So, we can't always change what we're going through, but we can make the most of every situation. How can you add some flirtation and sexiness back into your life? If your partner carries you to bed, maybe they can add in a good butt squeeze. Who doesn't like a good butt squeeze? You can have romantic nights in by soaking in a soothing bubble bath together. Candles, rose petals, and a bubble bath scream romance and, if you add in some Epsom salts, you'll be detoxing together (which might be gross now that I think about it… so please hop in the shower afterwards to rinse off all toxins)! Do you have some sexy lingerie? Sometimes the simple act of putting on something sexy can change your entire mood. Just like any relationship, it takes work to keep that spark going, and when you're battling Lyme, you might not always have the energy. So, do what you can, and do what makes you feel good. Feeling good is sexy in itself. And we all want more days filled with things that make us feel good! Yes, you'll have to make various adjustments while you're healing, but just because you're dealing with an illness does not mean the sexiness needs to go out the door. Find it and flaunt it, because you're so worth it.

The last thing I want to cover here is dealing with the trauma you may be carrying from past relationships. This is hard, and I do recommend therapy for the purpose of really working through these issues (because therapy is awesome), but here's my advice: No two people are the same, and we ourselves are ever-growing, -changing, and -evolving. Feelings aren't facts, so fearing a similar outcome before it's happened is not only unhealthy, but unrealistic. A broken heart is hard to mend and having fears around love is super normal and valid, especially if a previous relationship ended due to something related to Lyme. To repeat myself, the right person truly is not going to care whether you have Lyme disease or not. They are going to love you for *you* and so convincing *yourself* that you are more than your diagnosis will help you believe this. It's hard to do, but we have to find a way to open ourselves up again, in order to love and be loved! I'm not going to lie; it takes a strong person to date someone who battles an illness. But that's on them, not you. You deserve someone who is willing to join your fight, and don't settle for someone who isn't on board. Yes, give them grace, patience, and time, but the right person will get there. It's easier said than done, but the past is the past, and your new partner is not your old partner. And you've changed, too. In fact, time changes us all—and more often than not, for the better.

Being Single with Lyme

Okay, now that I've talked all about dating, if you're single (like I am right now), here's a chapter for you (us)! Being single can be awesome—and an important part of your healing journey. Here's why: When you're single you get to work solely on yourself, and you'll notice a whole lot of growth can and will happen. After all, you're stuck with yourself forever, so now's the perfect time to figure out who you are, who you want to be, and to make any necessary changes. When you're single, you get to fall in love with yourself, and I believe that itself can be a magical experience, if you're open to it. You might be thinking, "that's great for you, but I'd rather find my special someone right now," and I get it. I want that for myself, and for you as well! But keep in mind that this is just one chapter in your life. I don't know how long you'll be on your own over the course of your life, but we all go through it, and I encourage you to try to make the most of it.

Love happens only when you're able to love yourself. Do I love that I battle chronic Lyme disease? Not particularly. But am I grateful for the lessons and growth it's given me? Yes! It's normal to feel like you're missing out. I've watched a lot of my friends get engaged, married, have babies—all while I'm here taking supplements, doing treatments, and shitting parasites. Such fun! But really, this is my life right now, and maybe I'm not meant to have a partner in this current moment because I'm focusing on healing. Dating takes a lot of energy, and sometimes we need all the energy we have just to heal. It can be hard, but it's important to embrace living in the moment. Nothing ever stays the same, so just because you're single now, does not mean you'll be single in a month, a year, or five years from now. Then again, maybe you will. I've had extended periods of being single and it's not always fun, but it's also not the end of the world. Some people love the fact that they're single! You're not tied down; you're free to do whatever you want, whenever you want; and to focus all your energy on the most important person you'll ever meet: YOU. So, if you happen to be single as you're battling Lyme, know that you're not alone, it won't last forever, there's no shame in it, and it might be just what your body needs to heal.

Asking for Help

This is a hard step for so many Lyme warriors. I know it was for me. A lot of us have spent years of pretending we're okay because our symptoms are invisible; gone years without people believing us, so we felt we had no choice but to do things on our own. This can lead to putting up walls to protect ourselves but, in reality, these walls do more harm than good because they don't let others in when we desperately need help. Many of us fear the act of asking for help because we fear people saying "no." To us, it feels personal. For example, if I ask someone to walk my dog when I can't get out of bed, and they say "no," it hurts. I know it has nothing to do with me. I know their schedule simply didn't allow them to help but, for whatever reason, I'll still get offended because it *feels like* they don't really *want* to help. I can assure you, if that person is your friend, they do want to help you. But they are human, too, and it's important that they listen to their own needs and respect their own boundaries. So please, don't let one person's "no" stop you from asking for help. I've been there, so I know the temptation to say, "I'll just do it myself because it's easier than asking someone else and getting rejected!" I can assure you, though, that having this mindset will only last so long before you have a flare-up that leaves you feeling worse than before. This is why we build a support system, and assemble a team of helpers. We can't rely on one person to be there for us no matter what, although it's wonderful if you do have that one person! Everyone's got a busy life, and commitments can also come up unexpectedly, sometimes, so it's important that we continue to ask for help when one person says, "no." Usually, you'll find another person is able and willing to help, and it turns out to be a better situation for all involved. More simply: even if it's not the "yes" you were looking for, chances are you'll always have someone in your corner to be able to help when you need it. I've also had many people come to my aid without even asking! This is why it's important to vocalize your needs, so your support team knows when you're struggling. There are good people in the world, and many who are ready to help even when you haven't asked.

It's important for me to remind you that—as I've said before—just having "needs," doesn't make you "needy." Everyone has needs! It's universal! And, when you're dealing with a chronic illness, no matter how much you may want to fight it, you will need help. It's hard to come to the realization. Whether physical, emotional, or psychological, these are all normal needs for someone fighting Lyme disease. I'm going to be honest, I've also had a hard time letting people help me because I'm stubborn. Like my dad, I'm a fiercely independent and proud Greek American who would rather do things myself—even if it means watching my health plummet—than ask for assistance. That said, after years of suffering with this mentality, I realized that not asking for help was not only affecting me physically, but it was also affecting those around me. No one knew what I was dealing with, so no one knew I needed help. But when no one knows what you're going through, no one can even offer you help! In the end, it made the "ask" feel so much bigger than needed. So, if you find yourself hiding your story from everyone, try to find at least a few people to open up to about what you're going through. Those people are going to become your support system, and you might even find them offering to help you before you ask.

I also want to debunk here the idea that "asking for help makes you weak." Because, in reality, asking for help takes immense inner strength. As I've noted, our world is designed for able-bodied people, and society puts unrealistic expectations on everyone to just "push through." This attitude is harmful in more ways than one, but it's the world we live in right now. I know it's not easy to step into that vulnerable place and acknowledge when you can't do something on your own, but every person, chronic illness or not, needs help at one point or another. We're human. No one is invincible, no matter how strong they seem on the outside. And you know what? Ticks don't discriminate. Lyme disease has the ability to bring even the most indestructible person down. What you're going through is debilitating, but you aren't alone. Simply because you're fighting Lyme disease, I already view you as one of the strongest people in the world. And if you summon your ability to ask for help when you need it, you're well on your way to beating this disease and becoming a bigger, better person because of it.

Fear of Missing Out

FOMO is very, very real. But know that every person, Lyme warrior or not, deals with this fear. As humans, most of us fear the unknown; the "what ifs." And when you throw Lyme into the mix, everything gets heightened. There are actually a few fears I want to talk about that involve the fear of missing out: fear of not being included, fear of not being able to do something, and fear of never getting healthy.

Let's first start with that fear of not being included. As you know from getting this far in my book, friends may come and go, and even change, once you get diagnosed with Lyme disease. Your true friends won't go anywhere, but sometimes it takes a harsh wake-up call for you to see who can handle being by your side during difficult times. That said, even if all your friends stick around through your treatments, there's still a huge fear of not being invited to parties or hangouts ever again. At the height of your symptoms, you probably won't want to go to anything. So, you might find yourself declining invitations left and right, and that's okay. You'll be able to join in the fun again but here's the thing, if you step out of your friendship circle for a bit, you're also going to have to *actively* step back in. Your friends aren't going to know when you're feeling good vs. when you're feeling bad. You have to verbalize what's going on, and then show up. This process cannot be rushed. Some people need months to heal, and some need years. If you're the friend of a Lyme warrior reading this right now, it's okay to be unsure about how your friend feels. I encourage you to keep extending invitations their way, but I'll get into that more in a bit. People can and will change during the duration of their healing, yourself included! But by the time you're ready to venture out, you might find your group of friends no longer hangs out together, or doesn't do the same activities you once did. That's okay. It's all part of growing up. But the fear of never being included in something again needs to go because, whether your friend group changes or the activities change, you *are* going to get back into the world and have fun again. You're a good friend, and you're someone people want to hang out with, even as you fight Lyme disease! I hope you find amazing friends in the Lyme community like I have, because they're going to want to hang out (even if it's virtually) no matter what you're going through.

Now let's talk about that fear of not being able to do something. Physical and mental blocks often arise around an activity you used to do, but no longer can—or at least can't for the time being. There are certain circumstances where we must grieve activities that no longer suit our bodies, but as I've said before, I don't think anything is ever set in stone. The human body is so resilient, and the mind's neuroplasticity proves that people really can change, adapt, and grow. I've seen people get their lives back from brain rewiring programs and other Lyme treatments. People who were once bedbound, are now able to walk! Remember: no one can predict the future, and certainly don't ever let a doctor, or this diagnosis, dictate how you're going to live and what you're going to do.

To start, let's talk about activities that, for whatever reason, you can no longer take part in, right now. As Lyme warriors, we have to adapt to so many things in life, and sports are for sure one of them. Maybe you were a marathon runner, and Lyme has attacked your knees, making it impossible to run. I'm never going to say you won't be able to run again, but you might have to redefine your limits. Maybe it's a 5K instead of a marathon, or maybe you run assisted with braces and mobility aids, or maybe you use the elliptical instead of the treadmill. There isn't one definition for a sport! You can also still be involved in the sport without competing. You can volunteer at a race, or help train others from the sidelines. It's not the same, but it's still something.

If redefining your limits doesn't appeal to you, and you decide to give up that sport entirely, that's okay too. This happens. It's hard, and it was probably a big part of your life. Something you loved to do, and looked forward to doing every day. Lyme sucks, and I hate that it might have taken this away from you. So, you'll need to grieve what once was, and that might take a while. But, when you feel ready, I encourage you to take note of things you *can* do. It's time to adapt to your new reality and, in the process, you might even find something you love more than the original activity. Swimming, for instance, is a great low impact sport! But here's where a mental block might come into play. Let's say you despise swimming, or that you hate every sport except running. I'd ask you to take a beat and ask yourself whether you've ever given swimming a real chance. Maybe you're still in denial, or bitter about your situation? If you are, this is totally normal! And it might take years before you're able to accept things as they are. But in order to have a life you love, adapting and being open to change is how to move forward. It's not easy, but we have to embrace our "new normal" and be grateful for what we can do at any given moment. This is also a great time to try new hobbies! I've taken up painting again, and I adopted a puppy. I used to play tennis every week, and hit the gym nearly every day. I don't do that right now, because I know it's too much stress on my body while I'm going through treatments, but I've found other activities that bring me joy! And without battling Lyme, I don't think I would be painting or raising a dog who has become the light of my life.

Another big mental component around this fear is the concern we might have about incurring a flare-up if we push ourselves too hard. This is a very valid concern! But it's also a huge "what if," and we can't live our life in the "what if's" because that's all they are. Fears are not facts, and that dialogue looping through your head that's telling you "you can't do that!" needs to be debunked. There's no way to know whether, when you go on a hike with friends, you'll be bedbound for the remainder of that day. As I say again and again, you know your body best, and when you're deep into your healing, rest is super important. But when you're physically able to hike again, please don't let your brain scare you out of it! What we *think* becomes our *reality*, so if you're thinking you'll flare, you're actually more likely to. I also recognize that this is not something we can easily change. It takes time and a lot of effort to rewire these negative thinking patterns. But the best way to start overcoming these mental blocks is to take small steps in the right direction. If hiking is the goal, start with a walk around the block. Slowly increase your distance, as you're able to, and show your brain who the real boss is! When you're up for hiking again, it's always a good idea to schedule in a "rest day" afterwards, just in case, especially when you're first getting out there. You might not need it, but you'll be prepared if you do.

There are also very valid fears around "not being able to do something" that have nothing to do with bodily exertion. These fears can pop up around having the career you want. I've known many people who feel that Lyme has robbed them of their dreams, and I'll be the first person to say it's not fair. But like I mentioned above, I don't think any situation is truly permanent, and you deserve to have the career you love!

Besides, careers and dreams change for many reasons and circumstances that are out of our control—not just because of Lyme. But if you're feeling this way, the same steps apply as for physical limitations. Grieve, adapt, and move forward. Keep striving for a life you love, and remember that change isn't always bad! I'll give an example in my own life that I hope can clarify this a bit more: I'm currently writing this book, but I'm also making a pivot from my acting career. When I got diagnosed with Lyme, my life got turned upside down, and I've had to take a pause from acting. I realized it's time to tell my story rather than someone else's story. I'll share that memorizing lines was getting harder and harder. The long hours on set were too demanding for me. This has been hard. I do have a fear of not having the career I always dreamed about, and there are days when I get really angry at having to adapt. But then I stop, remember all that I'm grateful for and realize that it's okay to change. Acting will still be there if I ever decide to go back down that path. I don't know my future, but I can assure you that I'm going to make the most of my life, whether I'm an actor or not.

I've recently started both health-coaching and life-coaching classes, so I can give back and help others heal! I plan to create a healing community of my own with accountability classes and support groups. I feel very called to do this, alongside motivational speaking, and finishing my documentary about my healing journey. Life gave me Lyme, and I'm sure as hell making "Lyme-ade"! So, if you're finding that you need to change your career based on where you're at in your healing, it's okay and you aren't alone! Sometimes Lyme is the catalyst that makes you turn to a new career that actually brings you more joy than you ever could have imagined. I'm going to have an entire chapter on working with

Lyme, too. So, hold tight for that.

The last fear I'll discuss in this chapter is the "fear of never getting healthy." Often, this is a deep-rooted fear that, if you don't have yet, I hope you never develop. When you're healing from Lyme, it's often really hard to know that there are brighter days ahead. Battling Lyme is not only physically demanding, it's also the hardest thing I've ever gone through, mentally. Still, these fears aren't necessarily coming from *you*. It's the darn Lyme bacteria and other critters messing with your head! But you can still fight them and, as I've said before, it's vital to remember that FEELINGS AREN'T FACTS. And this includes fears! The fear of never getting healthy is just that, a fear, which is not a fact and therefore you cannot let it dictate your life. There are so many people who heal from Lyme disease, whether by reaching remission or something else. If they can do it, so can you. If it sometimes feels out of reach, I'm right there with you! But just because it hasn't happened yet, doesn't mean it never will.

As I've said many times: healing is possible, and I truly believe that everyone can reach remission, but there are some days where it just feels unattainable. When you're spiraling in a Lyme flare and can't see the light at the end of the tunnel, the last thing you want is for someone to keep telling you, "you're going to get better!" Because you're probably thinking, "WHEN am I going to get better? And WHY is this happening?"—both very valid feelings (which remember, are not facts). But they're real, and this shit is hard. I'm not going to sugarcoat it. Everyone's healing journey is different, and it's really hard to see someone else get better when it feels like you're not making any progress or, some days, even going backwards. But the best thing you can do is to let go of any expectations of how you will heal. So the treatment that worked for your friend isn't working for you? Let it go, it's not your path. Starting a new treatment that makes you sicker than ever and it just feels all wrong? Let it go and start something different if your doctor agrees that it wasn't the right protocol (or if you just know it's wrong, move on even if you disagree with your doctor). And thoughts about how you're going to heal in X amount of time? Let those go too! Some people heal within a few months, and others heal within a few years. There is no magical treatment or exact timeline for the way someone will heal from chronic Lyme disease. Once you're able to let go of your expectations about how and when you will heal, you might find that your health is actually starting to improve.

Finally, I want to say that there *is* life with Lyme disease! Many, many of us are living proof. Sometimes we get so caught up in worrying about our future that we forget to live right here, right now. We can't wait for life to get easy to find happiness! Yes, it's important to keep up your hope of healing, but there's so much life to be lived right now! Focusing on the present moment might even help squash those fearful thoughts. All we can do is live for today, work toward healing, and stay hopeful and strong no matter what's thrown our way.

Symptoms Can Change — And Come & Go

What I've learned from my own journey with chronic Lyme disease is that symptoms will come and go, things change, and nothing ever lasts forever. But it's true what they say, that when one door closes another one opens. Unfortunately, we sometimes have to hit rock bottom before this happens. But no matter what you're going through, there will be brighter days ahead. And days with less pain! The pain might not vanish, but there will be days when it will be bearable. I wish someone had told me this at the beginning of my Lyme journey.

Just like all the doctors I saw, I was dumbfounded by the way my symptoms came and went; and by the way new ones would pop up at random. Lyme can affect every single organ, muscle, and tissue in your body. As I've said several times, it also affects your brain because Borrelia burgdorferi breaks the blood-brain barrier. Cheeky little bacteria! So one of the biggest reasons I couldn't get the right diagnosis was because my symptoms kept changing. I had GI symptoms, so I went to a gastroenterologist, but they found nothing. Then I had heart palpitations, so I saw a cardiologist, and they found nothing. Then a urologist, neurologist, dentist, back specialist, etc.; you get the drill. New symptoms arose all the time and I thought, okay maybe *this* is the root cause of everything else! Nope. But you know what was? Lyme disease.

I think symptoms come and go because once you start peeling back the "onion" that is Lyme, something else (whether it be a co-infection, mold, or parasites) will start to surface. Also, Lyme disease can go into hiding. Again, cheeky little bacteria! So, if your symptoms are all over the place and every day seems different—maybe even every hour—you're not alone! These fluctuations are common with everyone I talk to who battles chronic Lyme. Just remember: As you start to detox and get the treatments that are right for your body, you'll notice you'll start to have more good days than bad.

And be aware that the coming and going of symptoms can happen before, during, or after treatment. I, for example, had years of insomnia, which is now gone! At the time, even the strongest sleep medications did not help but, years later, it just went away. The same thing happened with my chronic fatigue, headaches, cystic acne, and allergies. They just came and went. Other symptoms would stay persistent for a while, but that's Lyme—super unpredictable! As I've said before: healing is a marathon, not a race, and whatever you're fighting today does not decide how your tomorrow will be. I promise you that your symptoms will not last forever. Like I said above, they will change, come and go, and eventually, with the right treatments, get better. So, keep fighting the good fight. I'm fighting right alongside you! We're all in this together.

Surviving Flare-Ups

It might not seem like it in the moment, but I promise you, your flare-up WILL pass. Just like your symptoms won't last forever, neither will a flare. I can't tell you when, but after 12 years of fighting flare-ups, I can assure you that they will. Some of my flares lasted three days. That seemed to be the magic number before I started feeling well again. I remember my flare-ups arrived in a specific order, as well. The first day I would feel nauseous, the second day I would feel fatigued, and the third day I would feel pain all over. After hyperthermia treatments, I noticed my flare-ups would only last a few hours, instead of a few days. In fact, as I write this chapter, I'm recently out of a flare-up. Yesterday was rough, and I don't know what triggered it. People always ask me, "what did you eat?" because most people associate feeling nauseated with eating something that disagrees with you. Well, it's clear these folks don't have Lyme disease because though food *can* cause flare-ups, oftentimes they're triggered by nothing at all. I'd like to address how I've managed to get through flare-ups, and still keep living my life. The truth is, the longer you've been dealing with Lyme, the more coping strategies you have in your back pocket. But if you're recently diagnosed, you might not know where to start. So, here are a few tips that I hope will help you stay strong.

First, recognize a flare-up for what it is—that is, realize that it's happening—and rest. Sometimes, catching my flare early really helps, and other times it doesn't seem to matter. But overall, being *aware* will help you better prepare for the "fight." Now, I say "fight" in quotes because sometimes the best thing to do is nothing, i.e.: rest. But just because you're resting doesn't mean you aren't fighting extremely hard for your health! As I've said before, your body is fighting hard for YOU, so sometimes the best thing you can do is just rest and sleep. Remember, this is not doing nothing! Resting is an active choice on your end, and people who don't battle Lyme probably won't understand this. Sometimes we simply cannot "push through" like a healthy person can. Or, if we do that, we might be set back days or even weeks, whereas a healthier person might need one or two days to recover. It's just not worth it, and only you can choose to take care of yourself. Sometimes it's a hard choice to make, especially if your flare-up isn't that bad, or isn't bad right then. But setting a boundary is an act of self-love, and once you learn to work WITH your body and not AGAINST it, you'll learn to get through flare-ups easier and faster.

Next, try to take note of what your triggers might be, because many things can trigger flares—though don't stress about them, either. Flares can be triggered by foods, environmental toxins, the full moon, stress, and sometimes nothing at all. Let's look at the full moon, because it tends to affect most Lyme warriors. While this might sound "woo woo" again, I've experienced this to be true, myself. The world and our bodies are made up of energy and, during the full moon, the shift in the rhythm of the earth's atmosphere is said to produce more serotonin (which stimulates muscles), and less melatonin (which aids in sleep). This is the perfect environment for parasites to thrive, so it can help to do a parasite cleanse during this time. All this to say that our bodies, especially women's bodies, follow cycles. Yes, hormonally our periods can wreak havoc on our Lyme symptoms, but so can many things! Everyone is different and what triggers me won't necessarily trigger you, so I recommend keeping track of your daily symptoms, month by month. You can get a blank calendar or a journal, and write down everything you've felt during the day—the good and the bad. You might start to notice that you feel great at the beginning of the month, but terrible at the end. Your doctor or holistic practitioner can help you pinpoint why your body reacts to certain time periods. I don't have all the answers, but I can tell you that tracking your symptoms will give you peace of mind, and help you to prepare and plan ahead! I've had friends go as far as to make sure they aren't getting married during a full moon! It's a real thing, so I encourage you to be open to this wild phenomenon. It's worth noting, however, that tracking one's symptoms can tip into the realm of obsessive compulsive behavior, creating a lot of fear. For that reason, I no longer track my symptoms, but I did when I first started out! I also tracked, and will track, my symptoms if I'm starting a new protocol. If you do decide to track yours, just make a mental note of how you're feeling, and whether it's accidentally causing you anxiety. Everyone's different, so please do what's best for you.

Finally, once you've recognized the flare is happening and realized why (even if the answer is for no reason at all), it's then time to make a plan. I recommend using the same formula as for a Herxheimer reaction. You might be thinking, "what's the difference between a Herx and a flare"? That's a really good question! Honestly, there isn't a huge difference. Both can create debilitating symptoms, and often the same symptoms, usually due to increased inflammation in the body. But the main difference is that when you Herx, you're actively killing microbes—that is, you're in the middle of a treatment—whereas when you flare, you're not. Herxing happens when toxins die off, and that die off creates physical and mental symptoms. Flaring is when those toxins are being stirred up, for whatever reason, and are essentially having a party in your body. Both WILL pass; and binding, detoxing, and performing self-care can really help. Just to reiterate, here are some tips to use during a flare-up (or Herx reaction):

1. **Mentally prepare as best you can**, and have your support team's phone numbers handy because you might need to vent, or ask for help.

2. **Bind!** Take extra binders to soak up all of the toxins floating around your body.

3. **Detox!** Saunas, baths, and enemas can help flush out your symptoms.

4. **Stay positive.** Your flare-up will pass. After 12 years of battling them, I can assure you, they always do.

5. Focus on self-care and rest. Give your body and mind extra love, and choose to rest if you can.

Again, I can assure you that these reactions will pass, that you will get through this, and that it will get easier and better as you move forward on your journey. Stay strong, you are a warrior.

It's Okay to Take a Break!

No matter how strong you are, mentally and physically, your symptoms will come and go, you will have great days and terrible days. So sometimes we need a break, just to enjoy life, feed our souls, and even feed the bugs. This is going to be a controversial chapter, but as I've stated before, this is based on my journey and what's helped me. Take what resonates with you and leave what doesn't!

We fight so hard to get better, even before receiving a diagnosis, and the fight doesn't let up once we know what we've got and begin treatments. But, as I've said before, there is no magic pill or protocol that's guaranteed to heal chronic Lyme. Everything is trial and error, and that includes the duration of your treatments. So consult with your doctor before stopping any treatment, but you do know your body best—and when it comes to healing, your mental health and happiness is just as important as your physical health. Taking a break is not the same thing as stopping altogether, which you're also allowed to do, but hitting pause and regrouping can be an important part of your healing journey.

I've taken much needed breaks from medical treatments, not because stopping would make me feel better, but because I was so mentally drained that I needed to feel like a "normal" person for a while. At one point during this period, I was taking about 30 pills a day. This included antibiotics and a plethora of supplements. I was also doing IV treatments a few times a week and, frankly, attacking everything too hard and too fast. I couldn't take it. So, even though my desire to get better had always outweighed my desire to avoid negative side effects from treatments, sometimes too much is too much. We're all human, and there are limits to how much we can take. I was slow to believe this, though. I put my full trust in my doctor, the one who pushed me way too hard, and when I hit rock bottom and found myself in a deep depression, nearly bedbound and unable to function, I stopped everything for a full three months. Then, I found a new doctor who was a better fit. I felt so much better during those three months "on pause," and immediately knew I'd made the best choice for both my mental and physical health. I've also taken days or weeks off from specific treatments and found great relief from even a short break. I'm currently treating parasites, and even though the herbs are making me feel a lot better, I've also taken time off this summer to give my liver a break and my mental health a break. The pills aren't going anywhere! Sometimes I just need to hit pause; regroup; and live my life without feeling burdened by a strict pill schedule. Then, I pick back up and get to work.

Since my symptoms were mainly gastrointestinal, I also used to find relief in breaking my strict diet. I like to call it, "feeding the bugs." There were days where my stomach was in knots, and the die off and detox symptoms were just too much. Still, I noticed that when I ate some sugar, my symptoms got better. The critters in me crave sugar, so sometimes I'd go buy gummy bears, or have a chai latte, or maybe the gluten-free cookies I'd been avoiding! I never went on a rampage of unhealthy foods for very long, I usually just treated myself to one thing and then stuck with my healthy diet. But after fulfilling my body's sugar craving, I noticed a difference in how I felt, almost right away. Is there a mental aspect to this? Most definitely! Does it matter? Not at all! If my brain tells my body that drinking a chai latte will make me feel better, and it does, then that's wonderful. The brain is extremely powerful. But, whether I felt better because I told myself I'd feel better; or the drink fed the critters and incited a dance party in my gut doesn't matter. I felt better, and that was the goal. Also, I'm working on retraining my brain so it does not consider sugar to be the answer but, until I've mastered it, I will choose to occasionally feed the bugs—and my soul!

It's worth noting here that some people will advise you against taking breaks from treatments, and that's okay. Everyone is allowed to have their own opinion, but only you can decide what's best for you. Healing looks different for everyone, and everyone has a different threshold for discomfort and pain, so don't let anyone shame you for taking a break if it gives you relief. If a break makes you feel better or simply ALIVE, then go for it. I will repeat myself and ask that you please consult your doctor before stopping a specific treatment plan but, if no one else gives you permission to live a little, let me. We go through so much being chronically ill, we deserve to treat ourselves every now and again, and sometimes taking a break is exactly what our healing journey needs.

The Power of Thoughts & Words

The way we talk to ourselves, envision our futures, and think about our life, profoundly affects us. I think many people, myself included, forget just how powerful our words and thoughts really are. Our brains can't tell the difference between what is real and what is imaginary, and that's why manifestation can work so well—and why putting ourselves down can be so detrimental. Our brains can't tell the difference between an environmental stressor (mold, EMFs, etc.); an emotional stressor (negative thoughts, emotions, etc.); or a physical stressor (poor sleep, bad diet, injuries, etc.), so they believe it all. That's how our thoughts create some of the biggest problems in our lives! Here's how it works: When the limbic system becomes dysfunctional, we develop symptoms such as brain fog, anxiety, depression, digestive issues, pain, increased sensitivity to sound and light, and more. And sometimes, negative thinking patterns become hardwired into our brains. Here are some common negative thinking and speaking patterns you might identify with:

- Defining yourself by your diagnosis

- Constantly thinking about your symptoms & diagnosis

- Obsessively scanning your body for symptoms

- Complaining about your symptoms

- Blaming yourself for being sick

- Over-analyzing your health; obsessively tracking things like your weight, daily calorie count, hours of sleep, etc.

Brain rewiring can help you change these negative patterns! I highly encourage you to look into the practice (as I mentioned earlier, DNRS and the Gupta Program are great) but, in the meantime, here are some things I've found to help cultivate a positive and grateful mindset:

• If you find yourself criticizing your body, take a moment and ask yourself, "would I say these words about my best friend's body?"

• If you're predicting the future, such as deciding that the worst will happen, take a moment and ask yourself, "are these facts or feelings"? My guess is that they're feelings.

• Put your self-talk on "trial." When a thought bubbles up, ask yourself if you have any evidence to support it. Can you *prove* to yourself that everything you're saying is justified and true? If not, you know you're dealing with a feeling, not a fact.

• What do you hope your future will look like? As I've explained, our brains can't necessarily tell the difference between reality and fantasy, so the more you focus on the things you truly want, the more your brain will start to believe it's the truth. Visualizations are also really helpful! Try to make sure you incorporate all five of your senses when you do them, asking yourself, *where am I?*, *what am I doing?*, *what do I see, smell, and touch?*, and *how do I feel?*

• Remember to track how many times you focus on your symptoms every day because, if your symptoms are consuming your thoughts, how can your brain focus on healing? It can't. So, every time you start fixating on a certain symptom, try to picture what it will be like once you're living without it! And thank your body for fighting so hard for you.

Ultimately, we need to give less power to our thoughts about our symptoms, and more power to our thoughts about healing. Words are powerful, and can absolutely help you! Here are some great affirmations you can practice daily. Pick and choose which ones resonate with you, or write your own!

AFFIRMATIONS

I am healthy, happy, and whole.

I view myself as vibrantly strong and capable.

Resting is also a sign of strength.

I am worthy of everything my heart desires.

My life is full of meaning, and I have a purpose here on Earth.

I allow myself to give and receive love.

I feel grounded, safe, and secure in my body.

I am patient with my body—I know it's working to heal me.

I let go of needing to control my healing.

I am physically and emotionally connected to an abundant source of healing. It's always available to me.

I can do hard things, and I will face every battle!

Writing thoughts down can also be really helpful! Journaling not only helps us release the chaos in our minds, but it can also help us to manifest our future healthy selves. Here are some journal prompts I've found very helpful, and I hope they help you too!

JOURNAL PROMPTS

1. What will your life look like when you are completely healthy?

2. What will a perfect day look like when you feel great?

3. What is holding you back from that perfect day?

4. Can you modify your perfect day in a way that works for your body and mind in this present moment?

5. Write a love letter to yourself.

6. What are three things you're grateful for?

7. If your best friend had all of your Lyme symptoms, what would you say to make them feel better?

8. Review the advice you just gave your best friend, and now write it all down for yourself.

Stop Fearing the Worst

Do you ever jump to conclusions and imagine the worst-case scenario about something? This is really common for someone battling a chronic illness like Lyme disease. We know that Lyme can affect us neurologically and emotionally, and some of our terrible thoughts just seem SO real. I still fall into this pattern far more than I'd like to admit. Remember that the neurological symptoms of Lyme can cause extreme anxiety, and since the future of our health is a big unknown, that makes our doom and gloom thinking even more scary. If you find yourself catastrophizing, know that you aren't alone, and that imagining the worst never helps. Actually, it can hurt you in the long run. Here are some examples of things I've catastrophized, and ways I've coped with these feelings.

One time, when I had a bad Herxheimer reaction, my immediate thoughts were "I'm dying," and "this is going to kill me." First, if you find yourself thinking or saying this too, remember that your feelings are valid. Herxing can be really scary, and while it might physically feel like you are dying, you aren't. You know what is dying? The Lyme bacteria, co-infections, and other toxins in your body! Bye-bye bugs! I can laugh about it now, but during a bad episode, it's no laughing matter. I've actually gone to the ER from this kind of reaction, and sometimes it's completely necessary to seek medical help. But if you don't need it, here are a few ways to calm yourself when these terrible thoughts arise. First, think to yourself or ask a friend, "are my thoughts true?" Think of all the Lyme warriors out there who have Herxed. They didn't die from it. So how likely is it that your feeling is going to come true? Not likely, even though it may feel that way. Then you can ask, have I been in this situation before? If it's your first time experiencing a Herxheimer reaction, your answer is no, but I've Herxed more times than I can count, and I still had out-of-proportion fears around them. So, I try to think back and realize: you know, I've been in this situation before, and I did not die, and was instead fine again after a few hours, or by the next day.

Another common way that Lyme warriors (and people in general) catastrophize is by googling their symptoms. Do not do this! Honestly, every time I've googled a new symptom, it says I have cancer. Google is the best at spitting out catastrophizing information, and it will just make you spiral. We become so desperate for answers—I know this feeling all too well—but I can assure you that Google is not the way. Instead, when you start going down this path, I encourage you to reach out to the Lyme community, to a friend who gets it, or to your doctor to discuss what's going on. Make sure to connect with someone who understands Lyme, because if they don't, they'll most likely start googling it as well and only end up aiding in your catastrophizing! Lyme symptoms happen, they're weird, random, and frightening. You do not need to add any more stress to the situation when you can just as easily get some real answers from your medical team.

Many Lyme warriors will also catastrophize about being liked and judged. For instance, when someone doesn't respond to a text message right away, we may decide it's because this person hates us. Honestly, it seems ridiculous that I even have to write this, but not only have I felt this way, it's been voiced a lot in the Lyme community. When someone doesn't respond in a timely manner, or responds in a way we don't expect, our brains can make up crazy lies about the situation, and we will start to fear the worst. Thoughts like, "Oh my gosh, she read my Instagram message but didn't respond—she must be angry at me!" Okay, let's calm down a second. First, why would this person be angry at you? Second, haven't there been plenty of times when you didn't respond to someone right away? And third, how long has it been since you posted your message? Yes, I've grown apart from friends during my battle with Lyme, but people change and that's life. And, for the most part, the catastrophizing we do when a friend actually ignores us, a family member dismisses us, or a date ghosts us is just not based in reality. Our brains take the situations to the next level, and get us hyped up for no reason at all. I don't know what catastrophizing situation you're dealing with, but I can assure you, you most likely aren't dying right now, Google does not understand chronic Lyme disease, and you are loved by many, many people. I'm going to tell myself this very thing for the rest of the day, too.

Stuck in Fight or Flight

When we fear the worst, and are unable to make even the simplest decision, our bodies are actually stuck in fight or flight mode. Battling Lyme is traumatic, and our brains resort to survival mode in order to keep us safe. But the problem is, when we're dealing with a chronic illness, our brains often get stuck there, and can't get out. The fight or flight response is a natural one, but not for everyday situations. It's designed for when we encounter life-threatening situations, like a burglar in our house, or a viscous animal on the street. We are wired to fight, or flee for our lives. This goes all the way back to caveman days when we had way more such emergencies. As I've said before, our bodies are constantly trying to heal and repair, aka: save our lives. So we have to get out of fight or flight mode and reprogram our brains to know that we aren't in danger 24/7.

We need to reprogram our brains because when we stay in fight or flight mode, our bodies prioritize an "emergency" kind of survival, where normal functions like digestion, tissue repair, and hormone production are halted. The stress hormone cortisol spikes and our memories are affected, our heart rate increases, and our bladders and bowels may even lose control. You can see how detrimental it would be to live like this, day to day. Still, it's completely normal to get stuck in fight or flight mode! All of us do from time to time. In fact, I don't know a single Lyme warrior who hasn't been affected by the fight or flight response. I've talked about fighting and fleeing, but there are three more types of reactions that happen in this mode: freezing, flopping, and fawning, and they're rarely discussed.

If you don't fight or flee from a situation, you might find yourself freezing—unable to do anything. These situations aren't always tangible, but many times we battle our own thoughts and get stuck in this mode. The expression "like a deer in headlights" is a great analogy. Ever seen a deer in the middle of the road when you're driving, and it just stands there, staring at you? You'd think its response would be to run out of the way, but many times it doesn't. It freezes in that moment of peril, because that's what its brain told it to do. In the same way, when a body knows it can't fight something, and it doesn't have time to flee, it often just freezes; stunned in the moment where no decision can be made. We can feel frozen in time and helpless when this happens. You might find yourself freezing when it comes to making a decision. Even a simple decision, like "what should I wear today?" or, "what do I want to eat for dinner?" These are common examples of getting stuck in the freezing stage of fight or flight.

The fourth reaction you might find yourself in is flopping. This is similar to freezing, except it's when you do what you're told to do without any protest. Flopping happens when the brain's ability to process information gets shut off, and you act a bit like a zombie. Freezing can come across as daydreaming, but flopping is more like you're dead inside. It's as if you think that by "doing nothing," dilemmas will simply go away. So you end up shutting down as a way to protect yourself from what's really going on. This can be detrimental because your emotions will become trapped in your body, and it'll be nearly impossible for you to advocate for yourself. Avoiding our issues is never the answer, but when we're in the flop mode, it feels like the only way out. I can assure you however that it's not, and that you're just stuck in a mode of fight or flight.

The fifth and final variety of fight or flight is fawning. Do you feel like you're a people pleaser? Most Lyme warriors do, including me. Fawning is our body's way of avoiding conflict by appeasing others. If you have a hard time advocating for yourself at the doctor's office, or find you're not able to stick up for yourself when someone tells you that chronic Lyme disease doesn't exist, you're probably stuck in the fawning mode. It might not seem like the end of the world to be stuck here, but you're not living your life to the fullest when you are. Feeling like you have to constantly make others happy means you aren't being your authentic self. And when you aren't your authentic self, how can you possibly heal? Your body won't be able to figure out who you are, what you're going through, or whether you need help. If you're avoiding conflict by fawning, you're still feeling all those negative feelings, they just get stifled—locked inside your body, becoming more and more repressed. Over time, these mental blocks might become the reason you aren't getting better.

So, how can you get out of fight or flight? Retraining the brain is the best tool for this condition. You can follow a program, incorporate daily meditation into your life, and find ways to calm down the limbic system. I've worked with a holistic chiropractor who does neurological realignment, and he was able to help get me out. Doing energy work can really help, too. When our energy gets trapped in our bodies, we feel physical pain, so deep breathing and releasing any emotions we're holding onto will help get things flowing. Like I mentioned before, battling Lyme disease is traumatic, and we really have to address that trauma. Working with a certified trauma coach or therapist can help get you on the right path. Being able to recognize that you're stuck in fight or flight, and then taking an action to address it, will really help you on your journey to remission. There's also no shame if you find yourself stuck here. I can assure you, most people end up here again and again, because as I've said before: healing is not linear.

Laughing Out Lyme

I think most people underestimate the incredible healing benefits of laughter. Laughter is helping me heal, and it can help you, too. Did you know the average four-year-old laughs 300 times per day? Three hundred! It takes the average 40-year-old two months to laugh that many times. So, what happens when we grow up? We start to realize that life isn't as fun, or funny, as it once was. Adulting is really hard, and throw in a chronic illness like Lyme disease on top of that, and life can get dark. Lyme disease is no joke, but we have to find one! We have to laugh, we have to love, and we have to live—otherwise Lyme wins.

Laughter is scientifically proven to help aid in healing. It reduces stress, releases dopamine and serotonin (mood boosting endorphins), and pumps oxygen to your circulatory system. Not only is it scientifically proven to help you feel better, but did you know that fake laughter has the same healing benefits as real laughter? Our bodies cannot distinguish between the two! So, as I discussed earlier, even though I'm not a huge fan of the phrase "fake it till you make it," I do encourage you to "fake laugh" as often as possible, because the more you fake it, the more your body will become programed to laugh, and look for things you find funny. Even adding a simple smile to your meditations can go a long way toward helping you feel better.

So, how can you find the laughter when your life seems the exact opposite of laughable? I know what it's like to think in bleak terms because I've been there. I've been down that dark road of misery, depression, and feeling like my life didn't matter. It's important to feel everything you're feeling, because all of it is valid, but I also want you to know that these thoughts won't last forever. And the more you can make the active choice to find the joy and the funny, the more you'll find yourself on the path of healing, rather than the path of illness. So, sometimes, even when it feels impossible, we have to find ways to laugh. Here are my shortcuts to finding that laughter:

1. **Watch a funny movie or TV show.** If you're not laughing naturally, let your favorite characters on television help you. Ideally, this will be a TV show or movie that you know brings you joy—one that guarantees to find you laughing. For instance, I love cheesy rom-coms like *Bridesmaids*, especially the pooping scene when they're shopping for bridesmaid dresses! I can't not laugh when Melissa McCarthy shits in the sink. Not only is it hilarious, but…it's pretty relatable! If you've gotten this far in the

book, you know Lyme warriors talk a lot about pooping, and I for one have certainly pooped myself, so I have no problem laughing at how much "butt stuff" I've had to do in treatment. So, when I feel like shit, allowing myself to get caught up in a character's hilarious predicament helps me forget about my own symptoms, even just for a few minutes.

2. **Force yourself to laugh by doing "laughter yoga," by listening to music that makes you smile, or by simply getting weird.** We laugh when we're uncomfortable—it's natural—and honestly, it's so healing! Laughter yoga is hilarious, and you can follow along with videos on YouTube. It essentially forces you to really inhabit your body, and "fake laugh" until real laughter comes out. Sometimes I'll do a weird dance and think back to when I was 13, looking at myself in the mirror, pretending to be a Spice Girl. I also dance with my dog, and I laugh when she gets so excited that she'll run and jump on the couch…and then fall off.

3. **Lastly, laugh about your symptoms and your situation with a Lyme friend, or someone else who truly gets it.** Usually, I find talking about what I'm going through to be extremely helpful with releasing negative thoughts and, when you're chatting with a good friend, they're naturally going to want to help you find the funny! No one wants to stay in a negative mindset for too long. Now, some friends aren't good at cheering others up, so I encourage you to reach out to the friends that do. For me, poop is a daily conversation, especially as I've been

shitting worms for months now, and laughing about it with a friend helps me find the joy in what would be considered a pretty "shitty" situation. See what I did there? I've found it extremely helpful to laugh through things, knowing I'm not alone, and knowing that everything is going to get better.

There are countless ways to find laughter in your life, and what I find funny might not be what you find funny. I encourage you to lean into your own joy and laughter, and to make the active choice to live in the mindset of finding the funny. I laugh every day. Maybe not 300 times a day, but every day regardless. I make funny videos about Lyme disease and share them with the community to help boost people's moods. Laughter is a gift, and it's one of the key ways that I'm healing from Lyme disease. It's free, accessible, and beneficial for everyone! I hope you'll try finding the funny today, and know that laughing out Lyme can and will help you heal.

Working a Job & Healing from Lyme

Healing from Lyme is a full-time job, but many people aren't able to put their life on hold and focus only on healing. I get it! For many years, I worked as a Party Princess (an entertainer for kid's birthday parties), a nanny, an actor, and a personal assistant as I battled severe fatigue, nausea, joint pain, headaches, insomnia, GI issues, and more. It was terrible, but I had no answers. No one could get to the root of why I was so sick, so I kept pushing through. Once I got diagnosed, I was able to finally put my health first. That makes me one of the lucky ones because I've been able to work a bit from home as I've been healing, but temporarily moving back in with my parents really allowed me to put all my focus on getting better. My parents financially support me, and I'll be forever grateful for that. If you're in a similar situation, I encourage you to take this time to heal, because as I've said repeatedly: healing truly is a job in itself, and there's nothing more important than your health. And remember: changing your living situation in order to get more support never means you've "given up," or that you're a "failure." Just the opposite! Instead, once you give into the healing process, surrender your ego, and live in the present, you'll be fully able to heal. But, to those Lyme warriors who have to continue to work (as most do), here are a few things to keep in mind, that can help:

1. Generally, you do not have to tell your employer about your health situation, but I'm going to encourage you to. Disability, and employment, and workplace health and safety laws vary widely across the United States. So, should your Lyme symptoms start affecting the quality of your work in any way, it's likely in your best interest to share your diagnosis to bolster your protection under the Americans with Disabilities Act (and state corollaries). And if your symptoms raise the possibility of being a danger to yourself or others, you are legally bound to share that information (and may need to demonstrate to a physician that you can perform your duties and will not pose a danger to others in your workplace). I told my bosses about my health struggles right away, and they were incredibly supportive when I needed to take a day off, now and again. But I was a personal assistant, and had a very close relationship with them. Not everyone does. But disclosing at least part of what you're going through, and reading up on the disability laws in your city and state, gives you the chance to let your employer better accommodate your needs—including time off to go to the doctor. After all, your boss wants you to succeed—and he/she/they hired you for a reason. So, if they're completely in the dark about what you're going through, you might find it hard to advocate for yourself, so I hope you really consider your options.

2. If you're looking for work, or trying to find a new job that's conducive to your healing, here are my suggestions:

• Find something that allows you to work remotely, or part time. Many Lyme warriors battle fatigue, so being able to work from home, or part time from home, is a game changer. Hiring a "vocational rehabilitationist" can also help you figure out how to adapt your skills to your current state of health.

• Make a list of every job that inspires you, and of all the opportunities you can find that are similar. Forcing ourselves to get out of bed for a job we love is much easier than for a job we hate.

• Your next job does not have to be what you do for the rest of your life. If you need to do something to make ends meet while you pay for treatments and heal, then find something temporary with this in mind.

• Life changes, dreams change, and it's a gift to discover new passions along the way. So be open to all possibilities when it comes to work because, what you once dreamt of doing might no longer be a possibility, and that's okay. Just because something is a "no" right now, doesn't necessarily mean it'll be a "no" later. You might even find a job that you love more than the one you had before, but you have to be open in order to find it!

• Work does not define you, just like Lyme disease does not define you. So whatever job you end up getting, whether you love it or it's a place holder, know you are so much more than that label.

3. Schedule rest days on the weekends, and weeknights after work. Getting a good night's sleep is so important, and it's vital for healing. Try to go to bed around the same time every night, and to wake up around the same time every morning. While you're healing, I recommend skipping after-work happy hours and other weeknight events. Your body will thank you later, and your true friends will understand your need to rest. Of course, you can attend some, but I encourage you to choose wisely and put your healing first.

4. Eat healthy, and prep meals for the work week ahead of time. It's so easy to fall into the trap of eating whatever's most convenient on busy days, but that often means junk food because it's cheap and easy to find. But you are what you eat, so eat well! Bring your own food to work, and fuel your body with healthy nutrients because it needs the extra support right now.

5. Have a morning playlist and routine that gets you pumped and excited about the day. Maybe it's doing a little dance while you brush your teeth, singing along to your favorite artist when you get dressed, or doing some gratitude journaling and affirmations while you're drinking your coffee. All of this can help you get into a positive mindset for the day.

6. Leave a little bit early for work so you can arrive a few minutes before you need to be there. This will give you time to decompress from your commute, and mentally prepare yourself for the day. I've found rushing of any kind causes anxiety and stress, both of which can make you flare.

7. There is no shame in asking for help and advocating for your needs. This might include asking for an ergonomic chair or a standing desk at work; whichever helps you manage best. It can also mean commuting to work with a friend, talking to your boss about finding work you can do from home, or deciding to move in with a relative. If I lived in the same city as my parents while I was working, I for sure would have moved home to heal. Not only does it save a lot of money, but having that support is so helpful. Some steps you can take on your own include purchasing blue light glasses for work if you're staring at a computer all day; or noise cancelling headphones, to help you concentrate. And, I've said before, it's important to remember that all the stuff that comes with Lyme is *not* permanent. The only constant is change, and your future has endless possibilities!

8. We're often our own worst critic, and sometimes when we

think we're doing a bad job at work, it's really all in our head. Your skillset, and the value you bring to the table, is why your employer hired you. So try not to let the negative talk that goes on inside most of our minds fool you into thinking you're not doing a good job, or aren't doing enough. You were hired for a reason.

Social Media: Your Best Friend & Worst Enemy

Social media becomes a lifeline for many Lyme warriors! For all its downsides, I am still so grateful for it. But it's important to recognize social media's positives and negatives. I'm going to start with the good because I really do appreciate it, for all the connections I've made there. In my darkest moments, when I was living alone, it allowed me to call on the friends I made online.

Many people battling Lyme disease, or any chronic illness for that matter, feel utterly alone in their battles. Growing up, we make friends based on common interests, personality traits, who's in our classes at school, who lives in our neighborhood, and other such commonalities. For the most part, those friends don't usually have your illness, too. Or, if you're like me, you didn't know you had Lyme disease until much later in life. So, we go about the process of growing up by surrounding ourselves with people we love, but who might not necessarily understand the complexities of Lyme. And that's okay because, as I've said before, we are not this diagnosis! But there comes a time when you want, and even need, a community of fellow warriors. And that's where social media comes in.

Facebook, Instagram, Twitter, TikTok, YouTube, and whatever

new application comes out after this book is published—they're a way to connect with communities all around the world. Also, some people find themselves bedbound as they heal from Lyme, and social media is one way to connect with others without leaving the comfort of your home, or even bed. And what's so nice about our friends in Lyme communities, compared to the rest of our friends, is that they're made by choice, as opposed to circumstance. These people may not live in your town, and most likely don't do the same things you do, day in and day out. That's why social media can be such a wonderful tool, and now I finally have friends with chronic Lyme disease who really "get it."

Online Lyme communities are also a great way to watch other people's healing journeys, and to get inspired! When you don't see anyone in your day-to-day life healing from Lyme disease, how do you know it's possible? There's something special about actually watching this progress take place, versus just reading about it in a book, or being told about it in a doctor's office. Seeing my friends slowly but surely start to get better has been so encouraging to me and my healing journey, and I have social media to thank for that.

Now, there are a lot of downsides to social media that are really important to address, too. First and foremost, not everything you see on social media is real. People tend to post what they're like on their best days. So not only does our vision get skewed about other people's "realities," but now that the use of filters has become so excessive, a new beauty ideal has become even more unattainable. So, please, please, please do not believe everything you see on social media! And how can you tell when something's real and when it's not? Well, you can't always, so you need to remind yourself of social media's lack of reliability when scrolling through other people's feeds! I also encourage you to follow different types of people! Especially the Lyme warriors who post the good *and* the bad. The people who keep it real are the true inspirations out there. I aim to do this with my social media accounts but, again, no one is perfect. As I said earlier, even my default is also to post my most beautiful pictures. And there's no shame in doing so! We all deserve to feel attractive and loved, and we all have the right to post whatever we want.

It's also really important to take breaks from social media. Yes, social media might become your lifeline, but due to its inaccurate representations, you need to recognize that it is not, and cannot become, your reality. Also, the amount of internet trolls out there is ridiculous! If your profile is public, at one point or another there will be people you don't know, who feel the need to comment on your pictures and videos with their unsolicited opinions. As discussed earlier on, some online troll tells me that "chronic Lyme disease doesn't exist," just about every week. These comments hurt at first, but now I find them comical. My own self-worth is strong enough that when people make fun of Lyme disease, or even my looks and body, I know to just brush it off. But it took a lot of practice and long nights of crying before I realized that haters' and trolls' opinions don't matter. So, when you find yourself either looking for validation on social media, or becoming obsessed with unattainable beauty standards, it's time to take a break! It'll still be there when you're ready to come back.

Learning to Let Go

There's a lot that comes with "learning to let go," and it's all really important. Whether it's your Lyme diagnosis, a mean comment you received, being ghosted by a date, or even the fear of your future, it's important to get a grasp on why it's so vital to learn to let go. Holding a grudge about something or someone only affects you negatively in the long run. The other person, or whatever you're thinking about, is not dwelling over the issue like you are. And if they are, they also need to let it go. But for the most part, I think Lyme warriors struggle with this more than other people. So why is it so important for you to let things go?

As I've mentioned a few times, we hold emotions in our bodies, so the more we hold onto an issue, the more mentally and physically taxing it is. Going over something repeatedly in our head is not going to change the outcome of what happened, or what will happen in the future. It just causes unnecessary stress that could eventually make you flare. Stress is one of the biggest causes of a Lyme disease flare-up, and learning to let things go is one way to help avoid them. More often than not, the situations we stress about are much smaller than we imagine. Remember the chapter about jumping to conclusions and catastrophizing? This goes hand in hand with that. Because we can't always control our Lyme symptoms, many warriors feel the need to control other aspects of their lives. This is common, but we have to resist the urge. Life happens, and the better you can adapt to situations and "go with the flow," the more you'll start to see the bigger picture and realize that happiness comes when you aren't dwelling or obsessing.

So, how can you learn to let things go? As with many of the topics I've covered so far, it starts with a choice, and then it takes practice. What are some things that bring you joy? Or which people? Focus on everything good in your life, and dismiss whatever negative thought you're dwelling on. You can also tell yourself that you'll come back to the issue that's bothering you because sometimes all we need is a little time away from a problem to realize what the answer is. And the answer might be that it's not even a problem at all. Meditating on it, doing breathwork, and refocusing your attention on something else are other good ways to practice "letting it go." I also find that writing about an issue I'm dwelling on can be very cathartic. Sometimes we need to physically write down everything that's going on inside our mind, in order to let it go. You can write a letter to the person that hurt you, say every mean thing possible, and then rip it up or burn it. (Though if you burn it, please do it somewhere safe! I once filled my apartment with smoke because the letter didn't fully submerge in the water bowl! Whoops!) So vent about it, paint about it, write about it— do whatever you need to do in order to let it go. And then take a breath, smile, and move on.

I also want to quickly mention that sometimes these experiences we go through are opportunities for us to grow. When we can't simply "Let it Go", I like to think of another option, which is "Letting it Grow". Is there something we can learn from this situation? So, perhaps, if we encounter the same stressful experience in the future, we'll be able to better understand how to deal with it. Is there a lesson we're meant to learn? And perhaps, dare I say, is this happening for a reason and is actually an opportunity in disguise? Taking a step back and looking at the problem from a different point of view, might help you have a better understanding of what's truly going on. Whether you're letting it go, or letting it grow, either way you must find a way to move forward and not ruminate too long on the current issue.

Create Your Self-Care Tool Kit

This book is kind of a "tool kit" in itself, but having your own self-care "go to" list is really important. It'll be something you can turn to when you suddenly feel a flare coming on, or can't seem to get out of a flare, or simply need a pick me up. It'll be made of things you enjoy doing; things that make you feel loved, or calm; or whatever feeling you're looking to feel. I don't know what you enjoy doing, so I can't make one for you, but I can help get you started! Here are some ideas for what to put in your "self-care tool kit":

1. **Create a music playlist** (or a few). These can be songs that inspire and energize, that naturally make you want to sing and dance. There's so much healing power in music! Harness it! And listen to it as often as you need.

2. **Get a journal.** Whether you journal every day or not, you'll reach a point in your journey when you'll either be asked to journal about something, or you'll want to. I find journaling to be extremely cathartic, and so I always have a few stowed somewhere for when I want to vent, visualize, or dream.

3. **Make a Helper's List.** This is a list of friends who live nearby, who are willing and able to help you when you need it. There've

been times when I've been really sick, but couldn't think of any nearby friends to call. This was back when I felt weird about asking for help in general, and was so depressed that I didn't want to talk to anyone, anyway. This is when a Helper's List comes in handy. The people who make it onto this list get it, and want to be there for you. This list is a life saver, so have it close by and ready to use.

4. Buy your favorite movies and TV shows, or purchase a streaming device (or service) that has them. Watching your favorite movies and TV shows is a natural mood booster, and sometimes it's the only thing we want, or are able to do, in a given day. If you're too sick and fatigued to even have the energy to choose what to watch, grab your "go to" list and ask one of your friends to choose.

5. Stock up on your favorite comfort tools like essential oils, bath bombs, CBD oil, and heating pads. Personally, I love my electric blanket! But be sure to buy some things that help alleviate your pain, and have some extra supplies at home, in case you run out. This can also include your favorite supplements. For me, it's activated charcoal or some type of binder. Those can be self-care, too!

6. Stock up on your favorite healthy foods and drinks—but be sure they're ones you can tolerate. Flares can happen without warning, so it's important to have some essential food items on hand to get you through the day(s). For me, it's white rice, gluten-free waffles, electrolyte drinks, and chicken broth or bone broth. Before I knew I had Lyme disease, I kept ginger-ale and corn chips handy because they used to ease my flares. Symptoms change, cravings change, and diets change. This is all normal. So buy what helps YOU, and always have a little extra on hand.

7. Keep a fun activity that you can turn to for a boost, somewhere in your home. This could be a paint set, some good books, a coloring book, etc., as long as it's something you *love* to do, and are able to do. It can also take the form of fun apps on your phone. Whatever it is, this is your self-care list, and adding joy to your day is a huge component of self-care.

Strength Comes from the Struggle

Lyme warriors, I know what it feels like to want a quick and easy way to get your health back. You might be reading this book, able to relate to everything I'm talking about, but still be hoping for a simpler solution. This is totally normal and, many days, I still wish this for myself. This journey is HARD, but the last survival tip I want to talk about is the hardship itself. I want to share with you why I believe the struggle is important, and assure you that you are strong enough to manage it.

To start, I want you to picture the story of a caterpillar transforming into a butterfly. When the caterpillar is ready to evolve, it creates a cocoon, and slowly turns into a butterfly. But what most people don't think about is the journey this caterpillar takes, right inside the cocoon. If you were to cut the cocoon open when the butterfly is still inside, you'd find that the butterfly would drop to the ground and be unable to fly. The reason a butterfly can fly is because it gains strength every day that it's still in the cocoon. In fact, it can't even break out of the cocoon until it's got immense strength because that's what it takes for a butterfly to push its way out. A butterfly's wings become strong because of the struggle, and without that struggle, it can't fly.

The struggles you're facing as a Lyme warrior are likewise part of the process of healing. Each day you battle Lyme disease, you are becoming a stronger person, both mentally and physically. I call you a warrior because that's what you are. You wake up, day after day, despite the pain and suffering, and you battle for your health every second that you choose to keep going. You are gaining knowledge about your body, and about the many toxins in our world; and you have the perseverance to never give up, no matter how many obstacles you face; and you are grateful for every moment that you feel *healthy*. We become the most grateful people on this planet because we don't take a single thing for granted.

It might take you a while to come to these conclusions on your own because each person is at a different point in their journey. Reaching these realizations took me *years*, and I also don't feel this way every day. There are still some days when I just cry and scream and get angry about everything I'm going through. I'm allowed to feel all these emotions because no one said life is fair. But I always come back to my beliefs about this journey, and smile just knowing how strong I've become *because* of my struggles. Since battling chronic Lyme disease, I am more caring, understanding, and resilient. I cherish my life and the beauty of the world. I take in every sunrise and sunset I see, and feel gratitude for every day. Even during my worst days, I am grateful for the journey and excited about my healthy future ahead. Stay positive, my warrior friend, because we come out of this battle much stronger than when we began.

As I've said before: healing isn't easy, but it's so worth it.

Part Four: To Our Friends & Allies Who Don't Have Lyme

This final section is for those who don't have Lyme disease. It contains everything Lyme warriors would like you to know, but don't always say, and everything we hope you'll become more aware of, over time. May these chapters help you gain a better understanding of what we go through. And thank you in advance for your love and support!

Being Friends with a Chronically Ill Person

As I just said, people living with a chronic illness are some of the strongest people you'll ever meet. Who wouldn't want to be friends with a WARRIOR?! Unfortunately, some don't and, honestly, it's their loss. I've been battling chronic Lyme disease for the past 12 years, and I've seen a lot of people come and go, whether it was due to my Lyme symptoms or something else. We can't be everyone's cup of tea, and that's okay. Sometimes we grow up and grow apart, and that's also okay. I know how kind, smart, and funny I am, and if you don't want to be friends with this cool chick, then I'm not going to force you. But if you're lucky enough to be friends with a Lyme warrior, here are a few things that I'd love for you to know.

It usually comes down to the question, "how can you help?"—and the answer is probably different for everyone. I've thought about this a lot, and spoken with many chronically ill friends, and it really comes down to this: we'd like for you to listen, acknowledge, and sit with us in the pain; without trying to make it better. It means a lot when a friend can affirm that what we're going through sucks, encourage us to keep going, and lets us know that they'll be there for us through thick and thin. That doesn't mean we want you to "fix us." No one wants that. So, even if it's coming from a place of love, you have to let go of any desire you might have to help us "get better." It's not your job to do that. Yes, we all wish there was a magical pill that could cure us. We want it, and you want it for us. But, unfortunately, that pill does not exist, and we need to make the most out of our situation while we're going through it. When you attempt to "fix us," it feels like we aren't worthy just as we are. We have doctors we hire to help fix us, not friends. That means even if you think you have *the answer*, but your friend isn't open to hearing about it, it's just going to come across like you are forcing him/her/them to change, and it might even cause your friend to feel bitter. After I received the Lyme disease diagnosis, I still had a lot of friends try to diagnosis me with other illnesses because it didn't seem like I was getting better. Their "problem solving" came from a place of love but, the truth is, they didn't know what they were talking about, and it caused me a lot of anxiety. So, rather than dwelling on our symptoms, and trying to help us feel better all the time, try just *being with us* and accepting the symptoms—just as we must, for now. At the same time, encourage us to keep going without belittling what we're going through. These two things are what we really need. And thank you for caring so much, it really does mean a lot! But, sometimes, the best thing you can do for us is nothing at all. Though it's not really "nothing" now, is it? Your presence is powerful, and it's way more helpful than you'll ever know.

Oh, and please check in on us, because knowing we're thought about goes a long way. If our answer is "I can't talk right now," just remember we need you to be okay with that. I think many friends of chronically ill people get discouraged that the friendship becomes a one-way street for a while. And, honestly, it's fair and valid to feel that way. It's tough, and we know that. We don't blame you for it, but we will feel disappointed if you don't decide to stick it out. It takes a strong person to be there for someone else without anything in return. Friendships, just like relationships, aren't transactional and are rarely a perfect, 50/50 balance, anyway. The truth is that everyone brings something different to the table, and all friendships evolve over time. There are going to be days when plans get cancelled last minute, and things change at the drop of a dime. Trust me, it's as frustrating for us as it is for you. But putting our health first needs to be our priority, as we'd want you to do the same. When we have to change plans, please know it's not a "no," it's a "not right now."

Now, I'd like to explain why we can't always talk about our illness because it's an important topic and honestly, it has nothing to do with you. There are many reasons why we can't always talk about what's going on. I can't speak for every chronically ill person, but I'll share the experiences I've had around this issue. So, I'm an extrovert, and honestly, I LOVE talking! I love communicating with others, but sometimes I feel like a broken record. Whether I'm explaining my symptoms for the umpteenth time to the same person, or to a stranger, I still know that that person will never fully understand what I'm going through. It's also all I ever talk about with doctors, so it can be exhausting to go over my medical history again in personal relationships.

Also, I can't always verbally express the pain, frustration, and fear I have surrounding Lyme disease. Sometimes, talking about the truth makes this illness too real and, some days, I just want to live in an alternate universe where I'm not sick. At the end of the day, most chronically ill people want to be "normal" and "fit in." We don't always realize how beautiful it is to be unique. It takes a long time for us to view our illness as somewhat of a gift, and not a curse. So please don't force it. I promise you, we'll get there on our own.

Finally, I need to mention a strange dynamic that doesn't happen often, but one that's given me a weird feeling that's hard to wrap my head around, and that's the sensation of being someone's token "sick friend." Many people find joy in helping others, and that's wonderful but, at the end of the day, I am not my diagnosis. And some people have made me feel like battling Lyme is all I am. It's almost as if they enjoy the days when I'm sick, because they feel a sense of purpose in their life; i.e., helping me, and when I'm feeling healthy, they make me feel like I have to do a symptom check, which causes a lot of fear and anxiety. You see, I *am* going to heal from Lyme disease. I know I will and, once I do, I hope my friends will like me for *me*. Will I change throughout the journey? Most definitely. But I know I am changing for the better, and I hope my friends will have stuck around for the ride. I'll always be me, but I hope after years and years of being sick, I'll have become a more compassionate person than I was 12 years ago. I certainly know that I'm a more grateful person, because I never take a healthy day for granted. We all have "baggage," even you. But I would never say that baggage defines you, so please don't say your friend's illness defines them. Be friends because you like each other. You already know your friend has a lot of love to give, and if you stand by them during their dark days, the brighter ones are going to be that much brighter for you both.

Fatigue is Not the Same as Being Tired

As I said early on, we don't appreciate it when you equate your version of "feeling tired" to our fatigue. They're not the same, and I'd like to help you understand the difference. Fatigue makes us feel like our soul is being sucked out of our body, and it can come on at any time, for any reason. Even the most rest in the world will not cure our fatigue, nor will caffeine. I've found that fatigue just needs time to pass. Of course resting helps but usually even a nap won't fix fatigue. If someone is tired, they can drink some coffee or take a nap, and they'll usually feel better. On the outside, our fatigue might look like we're just really tired but, unfortunately, it's not as simple or straightforward as that.

So, when someone compares their "tired" to our fatigue, it's like a slap in the face; like our symptoms are being belittled. While it's likely an attempt to relate to how we feel, fatigue isn't like being tired at the end of a long day. If you want to know what fatigue feels like, picture pulling three all-nighters, and then falling down a flight of stairs. Our brain feels like mush, and pain radiates through every muscle of our body. We can't think clearly, our bodies are screaming for us to sleep whether we have time in our schedule or not, and the strongest pain meds often can't do a thing. Many Lyme warriors live in this state every single day. Some of us even work full time jobs like this. So, on days when you feel your absolute worst and are able to take a sick day from work, please remember that we don't get "sick days." Every day is a "sick day" when someone's battling Lyme disease.

So, what other things can you do when you're a caretaker of someone battling Lyme, or a family member or close friend who sees someone struggling, day in and day out? Try learning about The Spoon Theory (which I describe in "Learning to Rest"), so you understand that we have limited amounts of energy. Acknowledge our fatigue, and don't compare it to anything else. Don't try to force us to be positive, because sometimes we just need a good cry. Be with us in our pain and offer your support, not your advice. If you're a friend reading this, but you don't live with a Lyme warrior, making a phone call or sending a text just to check in, goes a long way.

Invite Us to Your Gatherings, Even if We Can't Come.

Many people start to assume that because we aren't drinking, or perhaps aren't leaving the house right now, that we don't want to get an invitation to an event. This isn't true! We often get excluded, and feel isolated, because friends go through this exact thought process and decide it'd be easier not to invite us. Well I'm here to tell you that even if someone's not drinking, they can still go to a bar and socialize with others. Now, some people might not want to do that, and that's totally fine too, but please allow us to voice our opinion before making the judgement for us! Also, getting an invitation to a party might be the one thing we're willing and able to leave our house for. The joy and excitement of having something to look forward to is huge for us! This said, as I mentioned earlier, we might still say no, or we might have to bail last minute, and if you understand anything about Lyme disease, you'll know we would never do that on purpose.

Now, what if you know we'll say no based on the kind of event it is, or you're not the host and can't extend an invitation? Please have a conversation with us! Sometimes I think people imagine that they're going to let me down if they say they're going to a party that I'm not invited to, or that they're hosting an event that I would not physically be able to attend, like a strenuous hike if I'm currently in treatment. Well, trust me, we'd rather have a conversation about it before seeing pictures of it on social media! Rather than going behind our backs, just try to be honest with us. We'd extend the same courtesy to you.

It's also helpful if you try to put yourself in our shoes. Imagine all of a sudden getting sick, and never getting better. Imagine being diagnosed with an illness, one that some people don't believe in and, all the while, your friends continue to gather together without inviting you. Imagine waking up and seeing pictures all over social media about the event, and knowing that not a single person reached out to you about it. You'd message one of your friends, wanting to talk about it, and they'd say, "we figured you would want to rest and didn't want to bother you." Most likely, you'd take this in, and express to them that actually, you would have *loved* to go because you were feeling well enough. They'd say "sorry, we'll definitely invite you next time," but then they don't. Again, and again, you miss out on events and slowly lose touch with the people you considered to be your best friends. Does this sound like some middle-school drama? Sometimes it really feels like it. And if this sounds unrealistic to you, I encourage you to help put an end to this type of false friendship. Remember: we might be sick, but we're not dead. If you hope to be invited to a party, please know we hope to, too.

Please Don't Give Unsolicited Advice

Have you ever offered advice to a friend before they asked for it? You're probably nodding your head right now and making a "whoops" face. This happens to everyone, not only to those with a friend who's got a chronic illness. We've all fallen into this trap. And I've certainly done this myself! Giving advice comes from a place of love, and a desire to help. The key word in this dynamic however is "unsolicited." If we don't ask for it, we don't necessarily want your advice. If you simply cannot contain yourself because of how amazing you believe your advice is, then please be okay with us saying, "we'll look into it," and just moving the conversation along. We love you, and we love how excited you get about our healing but, most likely, we've heard it all before.

I can't tell you how many times I've been asked whether I've tried "yoga, essential oils, meditation, or such-and-such new diet?" I wanna be like, "girl, I've been battling this invisible illness for over a decade. You really think I haven't tried all these things already?" If yoga was the answer, we'd all be cured by now! (But, yes, yoga is amazing; and it certainly does help a lot of people heal). Also, every person is different, and one person's healing journey is not the same as someone else's. So, while I'm thrilled that "X, Y, and Z" treatment worked for so-and-so, my personal battle with chronic Lyme disease is just that—*personal*. I'm not a statistic, and I'm not like anyone else.

We understand that you might have an innate desire to help us, and we'll never get angry at you for that. I simply hope that this chapter can help put into perspective how challenging it is to be on the receiving end of unsolicited advice. We're receiving guidance from our medical team,

Lyme support groups, and taking our own notes about who and what worked for the other warriors we meet. We have so much information we're trying to process, that adding the input of family and friends can feel overwhelming. It's simply having "too many cooks in the kitchen"! Now there'll be times when we *will* want your suggestions. Especially if we're changing doctors and seeking new treatments. If you're part of our support team, we certainly value your opinion, but when it comes to advice, I've found it's always best to at least ask your friend if they're open to hearing it.

Please Believe Us: Just Because You Can't See It, Doesn't Mean We Don't Feel It

To those who want to be an ally to Lyme warriors, it helps to remember that our symptoms are mostly invisible, and they can be hard for us to explain. We're very good at putting on a brave face because it's the only way we've been able to survive. But just because we look "okay," doesn't mean we feel okay. As I said earlier, comments like "you look great", or "you don't look sick," can actually be really hurtful. There are days I wished I looked as awful on the outside as I felt on the inside because then maybe, just maybe, people would be able to see how awful Lyme disease truly is.

So when I say, "please believe us," what I mean is, please don't make us feel like we have to keep explaining our symptoms, just to make you understand. If you really want to be an ally and friend, know that what we're going through is extremely difficult, and yet it often doesn't make sense, even to us. Don't dismiss our pain, or look confused if there's a day when we can't get out of bed. Please don't assume that just because we're at someone's party, looking like we're having a good time, that we're "cured." Likewise, don't presume that since our social media pictures show us smiling and looking happy we must feel better because, most likely, we don't.

I've gone to birthday parties, work functions, red carpet events, and more when I felt like absolute shit. But you better believe I put on some makeup, a stunning outfit, and faked a smile the entire night. Just because someone is chronically ill doesn't mean they aren't allowed to have a fun night out. Just because someone's out, and not sick in bed, doesn't mean they're suddenly 100% okay. Every day, people walk around carrying huge, invisible burdens, and that's why it's so important to never judge a book by its cover. Your friend might be depressed, yet you can't *see* those feelings. Someone you know might have cancer but, unless they're in treatment, you might never know. Everyone has battled something painful, so please be kind, and please believe someone when they say they're hurting, whether you can see it or not.

We Aren't Hysterical, We Have Lyme Rage

As I've noted before, Lyme disease affects the brain, and can cause intense neurological symptoms. Everyone experiences these differently, but many of us find we have sudden and drastic changes of emotion, which might make us seem hysterical or angry for no reason. This doesn't mean we can't and shouldn't be held accountable for our actions, but I hope this chapter will help family, friends, caretakers, and other allies look a bit more kindly on the person they know with Lyme who seems to have "anger issues."

166

When Lyme warriors do snap, I want you to know that it has less to do with you and more to do with the bacteria in our brains. Our emotions get heightened, especially when we're experiencing Herxheimer reactions, and we become irritable and angry, almost for no reason. But we *do* have a reason—and it's Lyme disease. So if we go from zero to 100 on the emotional scale, many times it's out of our control. We don't want to be angry and irritable, and we try really hard not to be, but sometimes we lash out at the strangest, and least appropriate, times.

Lyme rage can look as big as a blowout argument with someone we love, or as small as getting incredibly angry that the toast burnt. Really, the size of the issue doesn't matter because Lyme rage always makes us feel like it's "the end of the world." You might be thinking, "so what if the toast got burnt? Make more, or make something else!" The problem is, when we're battling Lyme rage, it doesn't feel as simple as that. We aren't rational in this state, so won't see that we can just make something else. We're pissed that we, or you, or whoever, burnt the toast because it's what we wanted, and we wanted it right then. Honestly, I feel like Lyme rage turns us into toddlers or hormonal teenagers. Our brains distort reality, and make even the smallest of things seem like a really big deal. This doesn't make up for the fact that we might have taken out our anger on you, but I hope this information gives you a little insight into why we sometimes act the way we do.

I can usually recognize Lyme rage after it happens, typically by the next day or so. In the moment, I just feel how I feel, and even if I try to step out of it and take note of my fury and "poor attitude," I usually can't change things up in the moment. I also want to note that this emotional instability can be frighteningly debilitating. It feels like someone else is controlling our brains. Many people even experience depersonalization when this happens, a sort of out-of-body experience, like we're watching the action from far outside, and can't do anything to stop it. In reality, it's really scary to watch ourselves lose control over our emotions. This said, with practice, mindfulness, and meditation, people find they're better able to manage Lyme rage. That's how it's been for me, and I consciously try to be at peace with the wild feelings, which means I take them out on other people less often. As we heal, Lyme rage diminishes. And while I never struggled with the issue daily, many Lyme warriors do. However often it affects someone, it is a real symptom, and it can be very difficult to navigate.

So, how can you be there for someone who's dealing with Lyme rage? The best thing is to try *not* to engage in an argument with us. We truly don't want to argue, but at times we can't seem to help it. If you can recognize Lyme rage, and not fire back or "feed the fire," it'll help avoid a silly argument. Putting your friend in check when they do this doesn't always help, either. You can call out their Lyme rage, but until their emotions have settled, they might not be able to recognize it the way you can. So, if you're able, try to give your friend grace when they lash out. They're going through a lot, and supporting them through these outbursts is the most helpful thing you can do. Ignoring an outburst works too because sometimes, we just have to cry it out, slam the door, and scream in your face. Eventually we move on, and hopefully soon enough to apologize, but until we can recognize the Lyme rage ourselves, it's best to just let it pass. And *thank you* for being the great ally you are and sticking through it—it means more to us than you know.

We Aren't Stupid, We Have Brain Fog

A few years ago, I bought a book titled something like "How Can I Get Smarter?" This was before I got diagnosed with Lyme, and I really thought that I was just losing my mind. I couldn't remember things, even forgetting how to spell some of the easiest words. I always got good grades in school but, to this day, I have a really hard time remembering the things I've learned, even in my favorite subjects. Some days, when I can't locate the TV remote, I'll end up finding it in the fridge. There are days when I can laugh about my brain fog because, when you find your phone tucked away in a tampon box, you can't help but laugh. But there are also days when it's really scary. Like when you're driving and can't remember where you're going, or what you're doing. Everyone deals with brain fog in their own way, some better than others, but all in all it's important to note that we aren't stupid.

We also aren't just forgetful. Lyme can actually cause dementia, and you wouldn't call someone "forgetful" who had that diagnosis, right? So remember that brain fog is exactly like it sounds. It makes us feel like we're lost in a fog, and we can't think clearly. Some days are worse than others and, like all storms, it does pass eventually. But when brain fog is at its worse, it's an incredible challenge. Forgetting the name of your best friend is terrifying, and this really does happen! Forgetting how to do simple math even though you took AP Calculus in high school, can freak you out. Some days we feel like a completely different person, and we'd give anything to go back to "normal." So, if you're like me and all of a sudden you start buying books on "how to get smarter," know that this isn't your fault—and if you watch a friend start to forget things, please don't make them feel inferior, or make fun of their intelligence. And don't laugh at them, unless they're laughing at themselves. Treating Lyme and its co-infections does help with this symptom, but feeling like you're losing your mind is really hard to deal with. And sometimes, we literally do begin to lose our minds. If Lyme goes untreated for too long, we absolutely can. In sum, brain fog is brutal, and at times debilitating, but it's also nothing to be ashamed of, and it *can* get better.

We Aren't Needy, We Have Needs

Getting diagnosed with chronic Lyme disease means taking on the long, and sometimes very difficult journey, of healing. Many of us have to completely upend our lives, diets, and careers; and make many more modifications along the way. It's a lot for us, and we know it's a lot for you as our friends, family, and caregivers. But many Lyme warriors won't ask you this favor, so I will. Please try to make modifications for us, too. Please try to alter your plans once in a while, so we can join. Please be sensitive to our food allergies by not making fun of our food restrictions, and don't tell us it's too hard to cater to our needs. If it seems difficult to you, please remember that we have to live like this every day, while you'll only need to make adjustments occasionally. I write this chapter because of my own, personal experience with being shut out of friend groups, no longer getting invited to join in activities, and having been forced to bring my own food to events because offering a gluten-free option was "too difficult." I've also had a lot of friends and family members do everything they can to include me. I'm extremely grateful for those people in my life and know how lucky that makes me, but not everyone has a support system like mine. I've also grieved broken friendships as I've mourned the loss of the person I once was. Trust me when I say that, while you might think it looks hard for us from the outside, we tend to hide the worst of it from view.

I also want to say, for the record, that some people get tired of making accommodations for us, especially over long periods of time. It's unfortunate, but it's true. So some friendships end because we've used up all of our "sick days," and it's just too much for someone to handle. If you're reading this as an ally, I implore you not to allow this to happen with your Lyme warrior friend. When I was first diagnosed and spent six full weeks at a medical facility, getting treatments, I got a lot of support from people I wasn't even expecting it from. I got very kind messages, and warm wishes hoping I'd get better soon. Not everyone receives this kind of behavior but, as I mentioned earlier, the messages also stopped just as quickly as they started. Whether people don't understand that our treatments can last years, or whether it simply becomes too much of a hassle to continue reaching out—it still hurts. I won't say this is okay, but I will say that many of us understand how difficult it can be for you.

We don't expect you to upend your lives the way we have. And, years on, most of us probably don't expect much from anyone. But if you want to be the best friend you can be, try to understand that we aren't trying to be needy, we simply have needs. We don't want to live with restrictions and modifications, but we have no choice. You do have a choice, though: to either help us, or not. We can't make that choice for you, and as I said before, not everyone can handle being friends with someone who's got a chronic illness. But we are human, just like you, and we're often desperate for friends, community, love, and compassion.

We'd give anything to have our old lives back, or to have more healthy days than sick ones. And most of all, we just want to be normal—to have normal problems, and normal social lives. But we can't when we're healing, because we're warriors facing battle. Our battles may be ours alone, but we'd love your support.

Friendships should be a two-way street, and I don't want to give the impression that someone battling Lyme has an excuse to be a shitty friend. We understand that we need to put the effort in, and reach out to you for help; to plan things, and to stay in contact. But when we're battling an illness day in and day out, we sometimes forget, or get consumed with our symptoms, or suffer from a brain fog that muddies our thinking. We aren't asking for a "free ride." And we aren't asking you to give up your own life in order to put us first. We aren't asking for phone calls every day, or even every week. But, as I've noted several times here, we ask that you remember us, consider our needs, and include us in activities when you can. Lyme disease is lonely, and we'd appreciate it so if you could help us feel less alone.

Be With Us in the Present Moment

A lot of Lyme warriors fear the future, as do many people, because it's a huge unknown. But for us, it's more than the usual, "where do you see yourself in five years?" It's more like, "will I be healthy enough in five years' time to live a 'normal' life"? Lyme warriors have dreams and goals just like everyone else. And just because we're sick doesn't mean that we don't want the things we once strived for. But, unfortunately, those dreams are no longer our number one priority. You know what is?

Staying alive, being able to walk, eating different types of food, remembering our friend's name, having the energy to take a shower, etc. When someone's in the thick of healing from Lyme disease, they desperately want the things that healthy people take for granted. Does that mean we want to talk about those things? No, not really. We hope you'll recognize our ongoing battle, and simply be with us wherever we are in the moment.

Many people ask me, "what're you going to do next?" or "what's your game plan?" or, "when do you think you'll get better?" All of these questions pertain to the future and if any of us knew precisely how we'd get better, I can assure you we'd be doing that right now. As I've said many times, Lyme treatments typically take months, or even years, before they yield any kind of improvement, and not every treatment works for everyone. Try to remember that we're doing the best we can, and if we have the strength, we'll tell you that right now, our plan is to heal. We don't know how or when this will happen, but we're working really hard to get there, and we'd appreciate it if you'd refrain from asking those types of questions till we do.

And, while the future is hard for us, the past is as well. Many of us remember what it was like before we got sick, and people born with Lyme can have an even harder time, thinking back. We all remember good times, healthy days, and fun adventures but even though they're happy memories, they can sometimes cause us to feel even worse about our current situation. Our "past self" might even feel like a different person to us, now. Yes, it's okay to reminisce, and some Lyme warriors might even want to. But overall, it's a good idea to keep things in the present, and not say things like "remember such-and-such time? I hope we can do that again." For now, just know that we hope so, too.

Sensitive Topics

As I've been describing, some topics are hard for us warriors to talk about. They're just too real and painful. Everyone's different, but I've found the following conversation topics to be especially difficult—and hard for others in the Lyme community, as well. That doesn't mean that we don't ever want to talk about them! Heck, I talk about some of them all the time, but it doesn't mean it's easy. So I'd encourage you to try to tread lightly around these topics, and recognize the impact they might have if you bring them up.

1. Dating, marriage, and kids. Most Lyme warriors I know want all three. Of course, not everyone does, but like everyone else, we want to love and be loved. But, as I wrote earlier, dating with a chronic illness is hard, and so it's not always easy for us to discuss, especially if we're single.

2. Working and having the career we always wanted. Some Lyme warriors go on to have their dream careers, and others stop working all together. Many of us end up changing careers in order to find a job that's suited to our needs, and many of us end up feeling like we don't even know what we want to do anymore. These changes are hard, and we often feel like we have to sacrifice our dreams in order to heal. Sometimes, we end up finding jobs we love far more than our previous jobs, but everyone's different. All I know is that working, and finding a purpose in life—all while healing from Lyme—is hard.

3. Weight loss or weight gain. Many Lyme warriors will lose and gain weight on their healing journeys. Inflammation can cause sudden weight gain, and parasites and food allergies can cause either, quite suddenly. I've had people joke and tell me, "I wish I were allergic to gluten, maybe I'd lose some weight too," and, "you were too skinny before, now you actually look healthy." Frankly, we don't care what the number on the scale says, we want to feel good and to fit in our clothes like everyone else. So please don't bring up our weight, especially if you don't know what's really going on.

4. Your medical opinions. As I've said more than once: everyone I meet seems to have an opinion about Lyme disease, including which treatments they think are the best. No matter our warrior differences, I'm guessing we're all literally sick and tired of people telling us how *they* think we ought to get better. We hear this from doctors, family members, and strangers on the internet. Whether you believe in Lyme disease or not, whether you think the treatments we're doing are "woo woo" or not—if you have nothing nice to say, kindly say nothing at all.

5. Your religious beliefs. Not everyone is religious, but shoving any of your personal beliefs down anyone's throat is an absolute "no." Before I got diagnosed, I was told more than once that prayer alone would heal me. As it happens, I'm a Christian, and I do believe in the power of prayer, but praying did not take my pain away, and I believe God has a bigger plan for me and my journey with Lyme disease. So, I get pretty annoyed when anyone tells me to "just pray about it." It's simply common courtesy to be respectful of others' beliefs, and that includes not forcing a "come to Jesus" moment on your friend who's battling Lyme. Frankly, many Lyme warriors I know end up feeling forgotten and forsaken by their families, friends, and whatever higher power they might believe in. I don't blame any of them for having religious doubts! I hope they'll all find a spiritual practice again but it's a personal decision, and it should never be based on anyone else's will.

We're Happy for You, But We're Sad for Ourselves

As I noted earlier on, I've watched a lot of my friends get engaged, married, have babies, find their dream career, etc., and I have been genuinely happy for them! That said, I'm also sad that I have yet to experience any of these things. So, if your friend battling Lyme doesn't seem as thrilled as you hoped by the announcement of your new achievement, it might be because it hurts a little more than you'd expect. Those of us with Lyme deal with loss and disappointment nearly every day. Our bodies don't function the way they're supposed to, and our brains make us feel anxious and depressed. I mean, no one *wants* to be sick. And I wouldn't wish Lyme disease on my worst enemy. Yet this is our life right now, and we're doing our best to function, stay positive, and be happy for others, all while feeling like we're completely falling apart. It's a lot to deal with, and the truth of the matter is, we're jealous.

We're jealous of your achievements, and so wish we could be celebrating our own milestones in life. We also wish we could be happier for you; we really do. But as I have said several times: we also want a normal, healthy, and happy life; and so anytime we see someone else getting that, it hurts. It hurts so deeply that we rarely let those feelings come to the surface. Not that we're asking for a pity party, or for you to lessen your joy! You deserve to feel everything you feel! But we're also allowed to feel everything we feel. It's just that, most of the time, we feel like we can't. People are "supposed" to be happy when their friends get engaged. We're supposed to ooh and aah at our friend's newborn child, or their latest success at work. That's what good friends do; we celebrate each other and root each other on. We warriors know that, and we do that, but deep down we'd give anything to be right where you are—and a part of us wishes you already knew that, too. So, if your friend who's battling Lyme seems a bit down after you announce something really exciting, this might be why. Of course, it's on us to process our own emotions and work through them, but I hope you can now understand how it might be hard for us to do so. All I'm asking is that you acknowledge this. You have a right to be upset if we aren't reacting the way you'd hoped, but at the same time, please try to understand us, because we're going through a lot.

This is not to say that you should avoid telling us your exciting news! Being kept out of the loop, on purpose, is far worse feeling than any jealousy that might arise. We're already so isolated as we battle Lyme, that the last thing we want is to find out about your success by seeing it on social media because you didn't want to hurt our feelings by telling us directly. After all, we're perfectly capable of feeling happy for someone else, even if we find it sad for ourselves. Honestly, we feel this way every day. I wrote this chapter in order to give you all a glimpse into how your friend might feel, especially if he/she/they don't tell you. But please don't hold this information against us. We're trying our best, and we want to be included, whether it hurts or not. We want to be the best friends we can be for you; it's just that sometimes, we may have some baggage to deal with—whether by ourselves, or in therapy—before we can fully express just how happy we are.

Care For Us, Consider Us — & Send Us Casseroles, Too

When you picture someone with a serious illness, it's common to think of someone who's got cancer, or something else with visible symptoms. And when that's the case, the person usually receives gift baskets, baked goods, and get-well cards. I don't mean to compare Lyme disease to cancer, because they're completely different beasts when it comes to illnesses, but I think that someone with chronic Lyme should be treated with the same kind of kindness and care. Lyme can be just as debilitating, and it can kill you. Yes. Did you know that? Probably not. Again, I'm not trying to compare Lyme and cancer, but I am trying to make the point that it shouldn't matter what the diagnosis is for someone to receive love and support.

If you learned of a loved one being diagnosed with cancer, you'd probably be sad, shocked, and devastated. Please believe me when I tell you that most people do not feel this way when their loved one gets diagnosed with chronic Lyme disease. They just don't. The magnitude of someone's illness shouldn't influence whether you're willing to step up and help them. But for whatever reason, Lyme gets put on the back burner. And after 12 years of suffering, I'm starting to understand more about *why* people dismiss this illness. Here are some of the realizations

I've made:

- As I noted earlier, the CDC does not acknowledge chronic Lyme disease as a condition, does not support its research or treatments, and therefore most Western doctors do not believe it's a credible illness.

- Some people think doctors, aka "White Coats," are akin to God and therefore assume they have all the answers. I can assure you they don't.

- Many people struggle to get a positive Lyme diagnosis because testing is highly inaccurate, and people aren't typically willing to believe that something is "real" without "proof."

- People can't always see the effects of Lyme, because our symptoms are often invisible. This makes it harder for people to believe that they're real.

- Most people go for years without a proper diagnosis; and most are able to function—to a degree—with this illness. Sometimes, we have no choice but to function, but that means that some people don't think we're as sick as we actually are.

- There is no clear treatment plan for chronic Lyme disease, because there has not been enough research or funding to establish one. And, since everyone's journey is different, what works for one person won't necessarily work for someone else.

To sum all this up, people tend to believe in what they can see, what they can understand, what they hear on the news, and what they're told by their doctors. There's a lot of misinformation about Lyme disease out there, but I can assure you that chronic Lyme is real, that it's terrible, and that we need your support. So, the next time you learn about someone getting diagnosed with chronic Lyme, please take it seriously and send them flowers or a card or a casserole. It's less about the material object than the thought behind it, so do what feels right to you. As someone who battles chronic Lyme every day, I know I'd be so grateful to receive any type of "get well soon" gift. It would show me that the sender acknowledges the seriousness of my illness, and that they're thinking of me and sending support. It's a simple gesture, but it goes a long way.

Diseases That Untreated Lyme Can Cause

I don't want this chapter to scare anyone, but I do hope it educates those who don't yet understand the full toll that chronic Lyme can take on the body. Chronic Lyme disease, especially if left untreated, can cause not only debilitating symptoms, but other illnesses, as well. First, as I've said before but will say again, Lyme disease is called "The Great Imitator" because it often gets misdiagnosed as fibromyalgia, rheumatoid arthritis, multiple sclerosis (MS), chronic fatigue syndrome; amyotrophic lateral sclerosis (ALS), aka Lou Gehrig's disease; lupus, and more. But it also has been shown to be the root cause of other diseases. That's because Lyme interferes with a multitude of biochemical processes in the body; it damages cells, creates inflammation, and causes a toxin overload, all of which can lead to some serious illnesses. There have been several studies noting that Lyme microbes, as well as other co-infections, mold, and parasites, have been linked to certain diseases and ailments. I'll mention a few of those studies below.

Board-certified pathologist, Alan B. MacDonald, M.D., found that Borrelia pathogens and parasites can cause devastating brain damage. In one of his studies[1], ten specimens provided by The Rocky Mountain Multiple Sclerosis Center Tissue Bank, showed that 10 out of 10 deceased MS patients showed evidence of Borrelia infected nematodes (intestinal worms). These infected worms were also found in five tissue specimens of people who died from Glioblastoma (brain cancer), and in four specimens who died from Lewy Body dementia.

Envita Medical Center in Scottdale, AZ, describes how Lyme disease patients can be more susceptible to cancer. They explain that a Borrelia bacteria infection has been shown to assist in tumor growth, cause inflammation, depress the immune system; and alter DNA, causing mutations in the cell. Dr. Dino Prato remarks that in a study[2] conducted at Envita, he and his co-authors found that over 90% of late-stage cancer patients had a Borrelia bacterial infection that contributed to the cancer.

Columbia University notes that mental health issues related to Lyme may go beyond depression, and even lead to suicide. Kathleen M. Pike, Ph.D., says that depression has been reported in up to 45% of patients with post-treatment Lyme symptoms. She also mentions that a case study[3] suggests that Lyme disease can be associated with symptoms

---

[1] Dr. Paul H. Dray Research Fellowship Endowment.

[2] Smith, A.J., Oertle, J. and Prato, D. 2014 "Cancer and Infectious Causes." *Open Journal of Medical Microbiology* 4: 161–177. https://dx.doi.org/10.4236/ojmm.2014.43019.

[3] David William Mattingley, Maju Mathew Koola. 2015. "Association of Lyme Disease and Schizoaffective Disorder, Bipolar Type: Is it Inflammation Mediated?" *Indian J Psychol Med*, 37, no. 2 (Apr–Jun): 243–246. https://doi.org/10.4103/0253-

related to schizophrenia, bipolar disorder, paranoia, delusions, hallucinations, and mania.

The CDC explains[4] that Lyme carditis occurs in approximately one out of every 100 Lyme disease cases reported to them. And from 1985 to 2019, there were 11 confirmed deaths worldwide due to Lyme carditis. Cardiologist Neica Goldberg, M.D., states that cardiac symptoms can happen if Lyme disease is left untreated, and can result in heart failure.

There are many other diseases that are being studied and found to relate back to Lyme disease, but I'm going to allow other medical and scientific books to explain this further. It's a fact that tick-borne diseases, and parasites and other toxic microbes, are the root cause of many human illnesses. What's scary is that Lyme disease can be dormant for anywhere from months to decades. Take me, for example. I was bit as a child, was relatively healthy throughout my teenage years, and then took a trip to Guatemala at age 19, and I've never been the same since. Lyme disease was essentially dormant in me for 10 years, and then it took me another 10 years to get diagnosed. So all it takes is one bite to change your life forever, and the sad reality is that too many people will never realize they have Lyme disease, until it's too late. There needs to be greater awareness, around the world, about how devastating this illness can be, and I hope anyone reading this book will join in the cause for better healthcare, testing, resources, funding, and treatment options!

7176.155660.

[4] Centers for Disease Control and Prevention, National Center for Emerging and Zoonotic Infectious Diseases (NCEZID), Division of Vector-Borne Diseases (DVBD).

Thank You for Being a Friend

If you don't hear this directly from your Lyme friend, take it from me, we have boundless thanks for you, and for all you do as a member of our support system. So THANK YOU for everything! Even if you've only realized how to be a warrior's friend from reading this book; the simple act of reading it, and wanting to understand what your friend is going through, is huge. No one's perfect, and we aren't asking for a perfect, unattainable friendship. We love you for who you are, and it's my hope that you'll love your warrior friend in the same way. So, when our best judgement goes out the door, maybe you can let compassion and understanding flood in. When we change plans last minute due to a flare-up, maybe the next activity you plan can be more inclusive of those with disabilities. And when your friend worries that their whole identity is Lyme, maybe you can acknowledge their disease, but remind them that they're so much more.

And to the caretakers of those battling Lyme, you are our heroes. Thank you for coming to our doctor appointments, for holding our hands as we receive results, for laughing with us and crying with us; and for emotionally, physically, and often financially supporting us, every single day. I can only imagine how draining it must be to watch someone you love going through this. And honestly, as a Lyme warrior myself, I don't say thank you enough to all of my friends and family who've stuck by my side. It can sometimes be hard to step back and acknowledge the help we're receiving because we're focusing all of our energy on surviving. But please know we are forever grateful for your love and support, for all you do, and we're sorry if we don't always verbalize it.

Friends and loved ones are sometimes the very reason we're able to keep going. The reason we get out of bed and fight to get better, and the reason we find joy along the way. When we can't love ourselves, you love us. When we can't help ourselves, you help us. And when we can't see a healthy future, you hold us, tell us we're perfect as we are, and assure us that healthier days are ahead. We look up to you like no one else, and the world would be a better place with more people like YOU in it.

Final Thoughts

Lyme disease is a terrible and often misunderstood illness, but it does not define our lives. We have to live, laugh, and love—otherwise, Lyme wins. As I've said multiple times in this book, I do believe we all can reach remission but, if we don't, our lives are still worth living. Lyme disease does not make us any less of a person, and I really hope that comes across in the pages you've read. I wrote *Tick Tock, It's LYME O'clock* with the hope of helping others but, in the end, it's helped me as well. I'm still healing, still paving my own path, and taking things day by day; some days, even hour by hour. And that's okay! Healing is about finding balance, patience, and most of all, gratitude. Most of these chapters are born from the "failures" I've experienced over the course of my healing journey but I persisted nonetheless, much like the Lyme bacteria. I failed, got up, failed, and got up again! I've learned from these downturns, and share them all so that others might bypass the same hardships. Still, enduring struggle is what builds strength, character, and community. And, if I can do it, so can you!

To everyone who's supported me along the way, thank you from the bottom of my heart. To anyone who didn't believe me, I forgive you. And to anyone who still doubts that chronic Lyme disease exists, I hope you never have to experience it yourself.